LEAPING OFF INTO SPACE

A Travel Guide to Risk and the Imagination

By
Janice L. DeRuiter, M.F.A.
and
Helen J. Shoemaker, Ph. D

Table of Contents

Introduction

Hana Highway, Maui, HI

About the Authors

Janice De Ruiter, MFA: My degree in creative writing and literature is from Mills College in Oakland, California. I was a poet–teacher with California Poets in the Schools from 1991 to 2004. Each poet with California Poets in the Schools must be published and trained. This organization has strict criteria that needs to be observed for the poet working for their organization.

My first experience in teaching poetry skills was with special-education classes in a high school. From there, I moved to working with a mentor teacher in poetry. This exposed me to several elementary schools. After that experience, I was asked to teach in local elementary schools on an ongoing basis. My work expanded to working with emotionally disturbed children, ages six to sixteen, in a special school setting where most of the students are residents of the facility. By the time I retired, I was working with more than four hundred students each school year.

For this book, I have tracked both first- and second-year students through one year of residencies. I have included examples of students I worked with in previous years and descriptions of their journey into the world of poetry.

Throughout the book, Ms. DeRuiter's portions will appear in roman type. Dr. Shoemaker's comments are presented in *italics*.

Helen Shoemaker, PhD: *My educational background and training have been in the areas of interdisciplinary human development, clinical counseling, and human science. Currently I am the director of Graduate programs in counseling psychology at Holy Names University in Oakland, CA. All of this helps to inform my passion for understanding the direct experiences of children so that together we might re-story their worlds in new and more life-enhancing ways. I am certain of the role creative expression can play in emotional healing, emotional and cognitive growth, and the development of consciousness, in general.*

Jan and I conceived of combining our areas of expertise and experience to examine thoughtfully the role of creativity in children's development as we understand it. This book is the result of our endeavor.

About the Book

We would like to tell you the story of a journey. We come from two different starting points. Janice DeRuiter is a poet and teacher who travels with a poetic mind and a suitcase full of words scrambling to become images. Helen Shoemaker is a director of graduate program in counseling psychology at Holy Names University in Oakland, California, who travels with a kaleidoscopic view of humans, taking into account their environment, experiences, and evolution.

We are inviting you to travel with us. Precisely where this journey begins and ends is yours to decide. No person ever experiences the same journey, even though they travel together. The vehicle that propels us through this particular journey is poetry. The journey is toward the world of imagination and includes how that world connects to our expanding sense of self as we grow and develop. This is not just any imagination, but yours and that of the children traveling with you, whether they are your own children or your students. In this book of our journey, there is a beginning and ending—a final stop, a destination. The book begins with setting the stage for how to discover and expand imagination. At various points of interest, the journey stops. We pause and look around. In each place, we explore the different landscapes that make up the world of poetry and how that world is reflected in our growth toward full potential. Every landscape has something to teach us about the techniques and habits of mind that set the stage for writing poetry and for propelling imagination into full reality. Each stop leads to another. The last stop of our journey requires the most risk. But like any journey you decide to take, you can change the itinerary to suit you. There really is no absolute path that leads to the world of the imagination and to the world of self. So if you want to, mix it up, change the stopping places. But do travel with us and help create your own story. To get ready, you need two pieces of luggage. One is a mind open to wonder—a mind ready to discover the links among creativity, poetry, and imagination in human development. The other piece is a journal. No journey is worthy of the name unless it is honored with a journal in which to capture the moments. So grab a notebook, a lovely writing journal, scraps of paper, and a pen or pencil, and get ready to record the story of your journey into the imagination.

Our guidebook for this journey has two sections. The first section, The Journey, contains two components. To show how the imagination can expand in a workshop setting, Ms. DeRuiter shares her workshop experience with several groups of students. Her voice in each chapter is under the heading, "From Classroom Experience" and is presented in roman type. The second component is Dr. Shoemaker's comments on the classroom experience from a developmental perspective. Her comments are under the heading "From a Developmental Perspective." These sections are in italics. At the end of each chapter there are two journaling suggestions. One is titled "For Your Writer's Journal. The other is titled "Journaling from a Development Perspective."

The second section of the book, "Practical Application in the Classroom" contains lesson plans giving you step-by-step directions for teaching each poetic technique. The lessons follow the same path of discovery as the preceding chapters. These lesson plans can be adapted for use with any age group. They've been used in various forms with children as young as eight and with adults both in college and already working. Chapter Ten is an introductory chapter. Beginning with Chapter Eleven each chapter follows a pattern. There is an introduction of the material to be presented. A section follows this on what is needed to prepare to teach the lesson. After that each lesson progresses as it is presented in the classroom. There is an explanation of the poetic tool. A presentation of the model poem follows next. This is followed by "Writing Time," "What You are Looking For," and an assignment. The assignment is presented in the format given to students.

From a Development Perspective

The beginnings of development can best be described as a newly formed mountain spring: clear, pure, energized, and ready to move, to flow, to gather, and to meet challenges that lie ahead. That spring turns into a small rivulet, with its path influenced by twigs, rocks, climate, and other environmental factors that impact its direction and movement.

All springs and small streams are unique and in motion. Participation as parents, teachers, and even strangers in the lives of children is as unpredictable and variable as the stream's environment. Furthermore, each individual child will react and respond by adjusting, moving, and changing in her own unique adaptations to what she perceives as her reality. Thus, the interactive path of development starts small—as the spring does—and moves forward. Adults are forces in the shaping of the child, and it is important to understand the nature of pre-puberty development, in general.

To better understand the crises of development that we all go through, Erikson provides a clear description.[1] The four crises of development he describes are the foundations of adult identity. The first crisis, Trust vs. Mistrust, happens during the first year of life, when the young Infant is dependent on primary caregivers for her every need. How the infant navigates through and comes to understand her experiences of the first year will influence her openness to the world and any new experiences. The successful resolution of this first and most fundamental developmental crisis carries an embodiment of hopefulness toward life. The child carries the resolution of this stage within her as she encounters and copes with the second developmental crisis, Autonomy vs. Shame and Doubt.

During the second developmental crisis, the child gains recognition of separateness from others and experiences personal intentionality and desire. When a bid for a cookie is not honored, the child begins to learn that, unfortunately, one's intentionality and desire are subjective, and important others do not necessarily share their meaning and value. Nevertheless, the child at two years of age is, in a sense, all will, with intentions to want to go a certain direction. When elders disagree with the child, she will fight for the right to be autonomous, seemingly (by the sounds of it) to the death. The child learns through the experience of this crisis that control over some aspects of existence, and over significant others, is infrequent. As he develops, the maturing person builds on early seeds of autonomy and learns to realize self-direction, negotiate with the world, make choices, and harness as well as integrate the creative aspects of wishing (or willfulness) with the more mature, conscious self-direction of willing.

The third developmental crisis, Initiative vs. Guilt, requires an integration of the resolutions of the first two crises. As the child moves into the preschool period, the developmental focus is on the act of energetic engagement, including reflecting, planning, initiating, and most importantly, imagining the self in motion. "[It is] an experience of the authentic self, one in which the body, the ego, and the self are experienced as harmonic, one in which the past, present, and future are integrated."[2]

---

[1] Erikson, 1963.

[2] R.T. Knowles, *Human Development and Human Possibility: Erikson in the Light of Heidegger* (New York: University Press of America, 1986), 100.

Around the time the child enters kindergarten or first grade, and continuing until the child reaches puberty, the resolutions of previous stages are influential as the child couples imagining and initiating strengths with increasingly greater skill development. The child joins ever-increasing levels of skill development with whatever tools are required (including her body) to accomplish personal intentions. As she masters various tasks, a sense of self as competent grows. This crisis is called "Industry vs. Inferiority." To better understand, let us consider learning to ride a bike here. The competent rider is not consumed with all the techniques of steering, pedaling, and balancing, but rather, when the self is engaged in an act of competence, the person rides the bike unconsciously. Should the crisis not be resolved successfully, often the child concentrates on the correct techniques required to accomplish the task but never quite feels in the flow of the experience of riding. Technique is important, but it is not the end point leading to self as competent. Rather, mastering technique is the beginning in the struggle toward competence.

As teachers and parents, our task is to guide children so that their unique qualities can develop successfully. The developing imagination is impacted by the process and outcome of each identified developmental crisis. For easy reference as you read this book, I have provided an overview of Erikson's developmental crises:

1. Trust vs. Mistrust (first year of life): As trust develops, it influences how open the child is to the world and any new experiences. This stage influences how willing the child is to take risks, for example.

2. Autonomy vs. Shame and Doubt (age two): Here the child gains recognition of her separateness from others and experiences her own intentions and desires. She learns how to direct impulses and how to make choices and begins to understand what is under her control and what is not.

3. Initiative vs. Guilt (pre-school): Each of the previous stages build on each other, and that unique resolution is the ground as the child's focus moves on to initiative vs. guilt. Here the child moves further toward autonomous function in the world as she takes her desires and what she has control over and submits it all to her plan. The child learns how to take initiative to execute the plan. This is the self in motion. One can understand how this stage can be more or less successful based on the resolution of the first two stages.

4. Industry vs. Inferiority (kindergarten to pre-adolescent): Finally, as a child moves forward from kindergarten toward puberty, she attempts to master various tasks until they become a part of herself. If she successfully masters a task, what once required focused concentration can be done unconsciously—e.g., the shift of beginning bike rider to competent rider who does all the coordinated movements without thinking.[3]

---

[3] Erikson, ibid.; Knowles, ibid.

SECTION I-THE JOURNEY

Chapter One
Leaping Off into Space:
Risk and the Imagination

Oregon Coast

From Classroom Experience

Like any journey, this one begins with the decision to leave behind the safety of what is familiar to us as we head for the adventure of new experiences. To use the imagination is to be willing to take a risk and try new things. By freeing up the imagination, we expose ourselves and in that exposure learn about ourselves in relationship to the world around us. I love to experiment with students to see what a new exercise will release. Much of the joy of being a poet is the freedom I feel to notice small things, to write words that spring from my mind without conscious thought. My major task as a writer in residence is to lead children into the adventure of the imagination. But at the beginning of each new session, I meet a familiar force.

I have to re-acquaint myself with risk as a palpable force, a shape, a persona. It breathes. Sometimes I can almost see it. Certainly I feel its immense presence. I can count on it being present on the first day of any residency. As a poet and a poet–teacher, I embrace risk. If I'm lucky, the children I work with let risk in with wild abandon.

Some children bang their heads against it, slam into its body, wailing, "I can't. I can't write. I have no ideas. I have no words." Their fears of not being able to do something "right" become a cage with no windows, with no cracks for their imaginations to creep through and begin to breathe into their creative lives.

So I pound against this invisible barrier until the sheer force of poetry's power shatters each individual cage into small fragments of images. The students begin to believe me when I say there is no way to be wrong when you write poetry—there is only *your* way. They must relinquish their searching for the rules that bind most of their lives. Trust grows, and they realize they don't have to worry about how to get a good grade. There are no grades to worry about. I don't use them. I use only praise for what is good and suggestions for how to make their writing better. The only way to be "wrong" is not to write at all.

From a Development Perspective

Nevertheless, I know that when children hold the belief that their academic struggles are permanent and they feel defined by them, they begin to give up. Over time, their internal language changes from "I have a problem in this area" to "I can't learn." Eventually, they cannot see themselves as separate from their difficulties—in a sense, the difficulties own them. If they are given the space to separate from these feelings

of inadequacy, they can begin to see their academic difficulties and fail-
ures as something separate from who they are. In this newly found spa-
ciousness, they can begin to see themselves as a person who sometimes
experiences problems and sometimes experiences successes. One way
to impact and potentially reverse the negative language of the self is to
create an atmosphere in which judgment is suspended, imagination is
freed up to breathe, and the child can begin to experience the self in a
new way.

From Classroom Experience

I suspect this is why resource and special education students suc-
ceed in poetry beyond what people expect for them. They no longer
hope for good grades. They have found a place where grades don't
matter. So hesitant words and large, careless letters formed by what
can only be called "creative spelling" trail across their pages. The stu-
dents stand up and read these treasures that have no way to be wrong.
One teenager's image sticks in my mind. He was part of a school for chil-
dren at risk—emotionally disturbed and living in a highly structured envi-
ronment. As is my habit, at the end of each session, I asked him if he was
willing to read his just-written poem to the class. This young man with
his glowing red hair came to the front of the room and sat in a chair. He
sighed a deep sigh full of fear. He struggled to get comfortable. Finally
the first uncertain words came from his unwilling tongue. Three words
into his poem, his nerves got the better of him. He stopped to take a
big breath. The students at this school are encouraged to verbalize their
emotions instead of acting out. This young man was learning. "This is so
hard for me," he muttered. One more deep sigh, and the words stuttered
forth again. Finally, many minutes later, while I felt myself tensing, trying
to breathe some confidence into him, he finished. He handed his poem,
which he had clutched in sweaty hands, to me with an admonition not to
lose it. I held the proof of his courageous journey. His classmates burst
into spontaneous applause. They knew the cost of his effort to read.

From a Development Perspective

When I think about this student from a developmental perspective,
in his risk-taking effort to reinvent himself, he personally held not only
his but the entire class's hopes and fears. This made it possible for the
class members to step back and to identify and experience some healing
of their own private, personal pain. With both hesitance and courage, he
made the immense effort to rewrite the language of the self—to separate
himself from a sense of shame and to begin to envision himself in a more
preferential way. In doing so, he opened himself to the process of healing

himself directly and created a situation that allowed classmates to mirror his process in their own psyches—absorbing and making their own the once-halting, but now functional, expression of freedom.

From Classroom Experience

To share your writing with another person, you have to be willing to open up a part of yourself that usually stays hidden—an often frightening first step. Each small encouragement lets you be willing to share more. But every time, there is a flutter of the heart beating to the rhythm of self-doubt—especially if you are used to rejection.

There is no formula to push, pull, or otherwise encourage students to take risks. A classroom poet, anyone working with children, has to invent techniques as each session develops. One child, one technique—there is no set way. One fourth-grader absolutely couldn't get any words down except her name in careful printing at the top of the page. She turned her back to the desk, folded her arms, bowed her bandana-covered head, and refused to write. Kneeling beside her, I reminded her that there was no way to be wrong except to not write at all. To try is to succeed. "The first line is the hardest," I said, spinning the familiar poet's encouragement out of my store of such lines. "No matter what it is, get one line down." Finally, she did. "I love horses" was the one line she wrote that first week.

"I love them, too," I said.

The next week, she bent her head to work, and I purposely didn't hover over her. I only gave in to a casual glance that showed me her pencil was moving. This line ended her poem: "I feel like a song that drifts to the ocean and beyond." The combination of a lesson on silence and the playing of unusual music released her mind to give forth a truly amazing poem.

From a Development Perspective

A basic sense of one's competence is a developmental milestone first achieved early in life. While adults may often revisit and question our competence in various life transitions, those early childhood feelings of competence or incompetence seem to form as crystals within us, giving us a perspective that either gains a greater firmness of belief through time, pressure, and the heat of living or is subject to change. If the opportunity is provided to dislodge any sedimentations of powerful negative self-assessment, a child may be freed from the powerful hold of earlier beliefs about the self. The creative process can provide just such an opportunity for each child to refigure the self. Unfortunately, the risk of being too vulnerable often weighs in heavily for the child who is making the decision to be open to the creative experience. It is a precarious moment.

The teacher must be there, acting as the stable bridge between the two worlds of the old self and the not-yet-new self of the child—the developmental edge. Sometimes that edge takes greater agility on the part of student and teacher, and sometimes it is like falling off the proverbial log.

From Classroom Experience

Students with a sense of self-confidence feel free to take risks from the very first day. One such poet wrote, "The colors fly from all objects." This is a perfect description for a first day spent outside under a gray sky with all the natural colors dimmed by the lack of sun.

Christine, a fourth grader, wrote the following:

I sit at my desk thinking of the clouds
and how they just sit there all day long
all fluffed up like cotton that's gray.
How it must feel to be a cloud all day
cold and wet and sitting still
and let the day just pass.

By the second lesson, I had already placed my secret code, a star, by Christine's name to tell me that she was a gifted writer. I do not know what small kernel pushes a person to write. All I really know is that to be a writer, you have to be willing to take risks. You have to toss your words out into the world and wait for an unknown editor to read them. But these writers are not adults; they are children who are still forming their creative identity. They need thoughtful encouragement to embrace risk taking. If you criticize a child's imaginative efforts, you plant a seed of doubt that grows into a weed that hinders growth. So before I read lines anonymously from the previous week's poems, I remind students that it is no reflection on their work if I don't read their poem. I read the poem of everyone in the class once, in a random order known only to myself. I tell them, "Your turn will come unless you don't write. If you don't try, I won't have anything of yours to read." And so we make our way through the entire class. Sometimes I struggle to find the beauty in words I can hardly read. Fortunately, each student usually has one line that reaches past his or her previous achievements. If all you get is one line, that is more than someone who never tries at all.

For Your Writer's Journal

Throughout these pages, we will never leave risk behind. Remember: To write is to risk, and to develop and grow into your full potential takes risk. As a poet–teacher, I repeat again and again, "If an image scares you, it is probably good." Grab your journal. Write what scares you. Think alarming thoughts. Surprise yourself. Let the word pictures roll off your pen, even if you're not sure that they have any meaning.

Journaling from a Development Perspective

In the West, "mandala" refers to the "personal world" in which one lives, the various elements of the mandala being the activities and interests in which one engages. The most important activity is at the center of the mandala, and the least important is at the periphery. Depicting one's personal mandala in pictorial form can give one a good indication of the state of one's spiritual life.[4] Ask yourself what is most important in your life. What holds the most meaning and value for you? Order these from most important to least, and start from the center with an image of the most important. Often, mandalas are circular in nature, but feel free to draw yours any shape you desire.

---

[4] Wikipedia, http://en.wikipedia.org/wiki/Mandala, accessed December 15, 2012.

Chapter Two
Metaphoric Madness

Southern Oregon Beach

From Classroom Experience

One thing any journey can guarantee us is the promise of leaving reality behind. Once the journey into the imagination has begun, the world in its familiar shape disappears. What possible relevance does this have for us in our everyday lives? No matter what endeavor we engage in—teaching, manufacturing, inventing, parenting, or technology—we need to be able to think in new and surprising ways. In short, we need creativity. Why use poetry to develop creativity? To answer that question, we need to look at some basic poetic tools.

To help students discover new ways of looking and thinking, I ask them early in a residency to leap with me into metaphoric madness. On a poetic level, metaphor helps the students write word pictures. What do I mean? Here's the mantra my students hear over and over again: "Your readers have to be able to paint a picture in their minds from your poem."

How do you go about creating metaphor? At its simplest level, metaphor is a comparison. A metaphor, using "is" or "of," is a comparison made true, whereas a simile uses "like" or "as." But beware, I don't mean Joe is as tall as Henry. That is a statement of fact. I'm asking for unusual connections. It is more visual and interesting for your reader if you use a simile or metaphor instead. "Standing tall like a light house on a point, Joe became a beacon of calm in the crowded room." Poets need to free their imagination to leap from one thing to something completely different and make them equal. They must turn their minds loose to let them go wherever they will.

From a Development Perspective

Freeing ourselves from conventional and sometimes restrictive thinking is generally more difficult with age and education. You may ask why. As we learn and are socialized into a particular culture, we begin to understand the world through a certain set of lenses—that of our family and friends and of authority figures. We are socialized into a particular set of thoughts, feelings, and behaviors, and we grow up believing that these are the only and right ways to think, feel, and act. Our freedoms are often severely mediated by these rules, yet the rules are invisible and often completely outside our awareness as inventions of culture rather than truth. We are born uncultivated, become accultur-ated quickly through our exposure to our culture's ways of being, and then spend much of the rest of our lives either assimilating to that mode of behavior or struggling against it. We often experience disequilibrium as we try to integrate experiences contrary to our current ways of being and knowing. Children are a little less fixed in their ways than adults and more open to new experiences. In fact, as teachers, we realize that it is often through the introduction of the novel that we can create the necessary cognitive dissonance, promoting a state of minor disequilibrium in a supportive holding environment, *enough to cause the child to take off the old "lenses," rub her eyes, and begin to see in a new way. One of the most difficult lenses to break through is the lens of productivity—the belief that every activity must lead, in both the long term and the short term, to production and that each of our goals should eventually move us toward being economically productive people. According to this way of thinking, any activity that is not "productive" is worthless, a useless waste of time. How important might it be, however, for children to "waste time"—to be less focused on productivity and more focused on the development of creativity?*

From Classroom Experience

One way to facilitate creative freedom is to play Poetry Ball, a ball game with words. Before I toss out the first word "ball," I tell students that the object of this game is to come up with two completely unrelated words and create a comparison from them. I pick the first word by using an object in the room so that there is something visual to begin with. Many times, I'll start with the word "desk." "Desk" becomes the first ball. To "catch" the ball and create their own word ball, students have to let a word pop into their heads, whether it makes sense or not. I encourage them to say the first word that comes to them. When they have a word, I tell them to raise their hands. When enough hands are raised to make it fun, I choose a student. It often happens at this point that the first word that pops out is really quite logical. So for now, "table" is the new ball. I point out that this is really a lot like a desk, so we need something wilder. Now the students must bounce off the word "table." It may take a few words for the connections to stop being logical. But sooner or later, the answers will get wild. One boy came up with the word "grass." When I get an answer like that, I stop quickly because I know we have the potential for a simile they can all visualize.

To end the game, they have to take two of the words and make a comparison, an unusual connection, using them. We'll use "desk" and "grass" to illustrate. You have to do something to both "desk" and "grass" to make them equal. So my question is, what do grass and a desk have in common? Puzzled frowns may greet this question. It's time for another question. What do you do at a desk? Someone may say "study." I push some more. What else do you do with a desk? Sit? Knowing I need more to get an image, I'll ask more questions. Can you sit on grass? What kinds of activities would involve sitting on grass? On this day, one answer was "picnic." At last, we had a shot at a great comparison.

At this point, I ask students to come up with a sentence comparing a desk to grass using the idea of a picnic. Obviously there is no one correct answer. "When I sit at my desk and study, it's like having a picnic for the mind" pops into my head, so I know I have an answer if they don't come up with one. Here's theirs: "Sitting at your desk at school and learning is like having a picnic on the grass at the park."

Yes, we are coming back to risk again. You must take a chance to create an unusual comparison. You also must look carefully at the smallest detail and be ready to let yourself accept the first crazy thought that enters your head. Several fourth-grade students studying poetry for their first year were successful. One wrote, "The grain of the wood I sit on/is like mazes on paper." Another wrote, "Pencils scratching like rabbits/burrowing in the dirt." And perhaps the most unusual was "Green hearts were falling off the trees." Still others struggled. "The pole is as still as the wind" and "The wind is blowing as cold as big hills on me" were other efforts.

The willingness to take risks doesn't get easier for some second-year students. Many are able to be free with new ideas from the beginning. Others, however, have to be encouraged to try all over again. They want to stay with the safety of lines like these: "The air is chilly./People get colds." Or "The leaf is brown./It's sharp on the edge." At least those two writers got in some details. Others still linger in a world of generalities—for example: "Houses are different colors and all different shapes."

From a Development Perspective

Moving beyond convention to creativity requires a willingness to be vulnerable—to be exposed as different, outside the norm. An engaged classroom provides the vehicle of legitimacy so the risk is less great, allowing students as a group to begin to see the world as metaphor. Without group consensus to engage them, elementary-aged students would struggle to give themselves permission to risk activation of the imagination. This is what the arts in general, and in this case poetry, potentially can provide to students: activation of the imagination made common. The classroom is a perfect vehicle for authorization of creativity. For some students, it happens easily and quickly, and for others, it is truly a moment of cognitive development in the sense of Vygotsky. Vygotsky believed that our higher mental functions begin and are further developed in interactive, social environments such as classrooms. He used the term "process activity" to illustrate that intelligence is not static but formed by stimulation and by each individual's social interaction.

From Classroom Experience

Some students are comfortable from the very first day with risks and the altered reality of creativity. "Silver drops/of anger cover me like/the icy chill of winter." Another careful observer wrote, "The sky is a beautiful wisdom/with treasures it holds within." The belief that everyone can be encouraged to explore the world using imagination is the force behind the willingness to spend hours with students and their poems.

Like all teachers, I depend on repetition to help students remember. So when I read lines from student poems anonymously, I ask the class to identify the poetic tools. First-year students (those in the fourth grade) have trouble recognizing metaphor or simile even when they hear the obvious "like" or "as." I have to keep giving them hints to draw them out. Perhaps it is the naming that is difficult. After all, "metaphor" and "simile" are not common words. Still, I encourage students to remember them.

If a class is having trouble recognizing comparisons in the poems, I'll have someone volunteer to create one on the spot. One such young man, a second-year student, gave this as an example of simile: "The windows of the cafeteria watch me like little eyes." Later in the lesson, he wanted to write under the table to gain a new perspective. He had the idea of looking at the world in new ways. Unfortunately, if I had let him go under the table, thirty others would follow, and chaos would have been the only result.

Resist the creeping thoughts that tell you that you're not creative. We all are. It's there from our first breath. Creativity's confinement in the necessary logic of everyday reality has to be released on a regular basis. Even for someone who appears to be a natural, the gift of imagination can get buried under the constant daily need to get through the day, to get everything done. Like anything else, the imagination needs nourishment and space to grow. If children are given the opportunity to sit still, be silent, and observe all the small wonders around them, they become so enraptured that they sit and stare in a timeless, trance-like state. When I tell parents at poetry readings how our poems were gathered from still moments outside, they comment that it has never occurred to them to sit outside quietly and just look. Like small children with a new toy, they, too, can't wait to try it.

For Your Writer's Journal

Grab small moments; even if it's as small a moment as coming out of a mall into twilight. Thinking only of the need to hurry, suddenly you're stopped by a crescent moon and by Venus hanging like a jewel in that rare, blue-black, twilight sky approaching lavender. Stop. Really look.

Take a "mind picture" and treasure it on your journey home. In your journaling, practice to escape your fast-moving collection of logical thought.

Journaling from a Development Perspective

It is time to grab your journal and visit an outdoor space where you have not been during those few moments right at dawn or dusk. This place may be very familiar to you at other times of day or night, but seeing it in transition may give you a new perspective, a new sense of yourself in that place. Follow any animals. Do they notice you? Can you engage them with soft sounds or your gaze? Fix your eyes on a tree's transformation of color. Notice the shapes of the spaces between the branches. Notice your skin and the air, complete with scents. What are you seeing in a new way? What do you know differently? What do you remember from another time in your life? How is this transition from night to day and day to night a metaphor for some aspect of your life's transformational moments? Present–past? Present–future?

Chapter Three
Exploring Silence

Southern Oregon Beach

From Classroom Experience

Our task is to travel into a still place beyond sound. It seems easy to observe your environment using the five senses: touch, taste, sight, hearing, and smell. Writers use all of their senses. A good writer needs to leave behind basic sensory input and discover what isn't easily observable. I've found that the challenge in working with young writers to be that we rarely experience silence in our world, and if we do, our tendency is to fill it with sound.

The noise of the world and the noise of our own minds weave together until silence becomes unimaginable and strange. How can there be silence in the midst of noise? You have to create it yourself. How well this works in the classroom depends on how a group of children assigned to a class interact together and how the class as a unit handles silence. I sometimes ask a class to sit quietly and just listen to what we hear. No one is to make a sound. No one is to move. Four out of five classes this year were able to be so quiet we could hear computers hum, the crinkling of pants as children moved, the unconscious tapping of feet and pencils, and even my creaking new shoes.

From a Development Perspective

In our waking moments, we are unconsciously making sense of the sounds of our world. Some sounds are easily, almost automatically, identified. Instant categorization of sound in the present relieves our minds so we can attend to other thoughts, usually about the past or future. We do not really hear *the present sound except to analyze—to interpret without much noticing—auditory nuances, without acknowledging that the particular perception of those nuances is unique to us. We hold an illusion that the perception of sound is the same—common and shared among humans—because often the labeling* of the sound *is the same. Yet all of us perceive our worlds differently through sound or any other of the five senses. One thing we do share as humans in this culture is that if the sound, or any sensation, does not cause us to accommodate, we barely notice it as sensory data. We quickly make sense without exploration. Perhaps invoking a personal stillness allows us to really perceive the nuances of sensation. But are we actually able to quiet our minds, to become still, internally?*

From Classroom Experience

I haven't forgotten the one class who couldn't be silent. I probably never will. It was a class for Gifted and Talented Education. This particular group was gifted in chaos. Yet some amazing poems resulted because some of the students were able to block the noise and write. A fifth-grader, Iesia, gave word pictures that captured the room: "Silence like a beautiful sunset/scratching of pencils echoes/...spitballs fly like hummingbirds following their prey." David, also in the fifth grade, wrote, "The monotone of light echoes/like a wolf howling...the annoying people laughing as music/ gives its secrets of love, hate, joy, and sorrow."

It was the silent classes that discovered the true experience of silence. They were all fourth-graders in their first year of poetry. Amy wrote, "Noise fades/silence grows/...my idea/flies away/a race/takes over my head." From Jessica: "Silence is a whole new world around./You can see darkness/in your mind/and thoughts sound like a beating/drum ringing in your head." Spencer created these lines: "A soft soothing music passes my ears/a song caught in my heart/words follow me/around the room/a song stuck in my head." Paul caught the idea of silence with these words: "Silence is a new way of things." Christine felt silence: "You feel like nothing is around you./There's a sound./It takes you out of your mind./It seems like it screams in your ear." Camille will continue to listen because she discovered that "The earth is my radio." Lauren broke into the world of silence with this description: "I fall through space/twirling/with the sound/of silence."

When I enter the poetry world of silence with students in their second year of workshops (fifth-grade students), I wonder what will be waiting for me. Will they be as willing to follow where I lead? Will I be able to build on their first-year experience? What new challenges will I face? In what way will they remember what we discovered the previous year?

From a Development Perspective

For a teacher, creating a stimulating and emotionally safe environment requires a personal ability to take risks and be vulnerable—the ability to open herself to new thoughts. The risks for her are greater than for her students. Will students engage? Will she be able to justify this approach to her principal? Can she use this vehicle to teach to the educational standards established for her grade? Will this educational endeavor promote development on many levels, especially cognitive, emotional, and ethical? Do you question "ethical"? Helping children expand the ways in which they see the world and the "different other" can eventually lead children out *of typical concrete thinking that is black and white and foster in the child the ability to look at an individual or a belief system* from a different and more expansive perspective. Fostering our own creativity will also challenge our current structures of thinking. Examining these structures can be difficult and requires courage. The development of creativity is more than just thinking outside the box in situations in which it may be useful or productive. Rather, it promotes living outside the box in our day-to-day lives so that we can move beyond dualistic thinking to entertain the complexity of every aspect of life and make more meaningful choices. This ethical development is useful to us as interconnected humans on a shrinking planet. If we cease to develop beyond the concrete operations stage of cognitive development, as so many adults have, our understanding freezes at a stage of simplicity. Certainly development is a lifelong possibility, but the risks to develop beyond one's set of engrained beliefs or cognitive structures is far more difficult when one has built his or her identity and social life on the foundation of such structures. A child's identity is being refigured daily, and a child's social world is ever expanding. Within this context, a child's sense of the ethical can be reformulated if she is given an opportunity to develop her interpretive structures toward a greater degree of complexity. Can you begin to see, in the following example, how this could happen?

From Classroom Experience

When we approached silence, surprise struck. I wanted to present silence and its counterpart sound in a different way. My second-year classes became a living experiment for how different sounds affect us and whether any student is able to create silence within. The previous year, they had been outside and silent. I wanted to expand on that experience and see how far they could "travel" with me. For part of the lesson, I deliberately played music that can be described only as irritating. Alex wrote, "I can't stand it/echoes coming from the/air itself/ bouncing in deep, slow/vibrations/shaking my ear to its limits." No less troubled by these discordant sounds, Katie wrote, "Seeps in my brain/like poison intoxicating my/thoughts and movements/sucks at my imagination/like leeches at blood/...I am a spring coiled/tightly if tripped/explosions of fury will/erupt."

During that same session, I alternated irritating music with soothing music. Then images shifted, and awareness changed. Alysha traveled into a place where silence was "so thick/so delicate/that a deep breath/will shatter it/into a thousand pieces /...don't close your eyes/don't let go/or you'll never come back/from the world of silence." Yes, students arrive in a completely other place: a landscape separated from the world of reality by a dense fog that waits for a moment of freedom from the normal boundaries of perception before it scatters and reveals its secrets. They are secrets like the one discovered by Paul: "So dark there is no sound/ no sound none/walk around in my own world of silence." In his secret place, Anthony found that "the wind blows like a/guitar's vibration." For a significant number of students, this experiment led them into a private space where their perceptions were altered.

In the final analysis, this may be what I most long for my students to discover. Our world is so much more than the surface. Around us lies a layer of reality that waits to be penetrated. For myself and also for the students I've worked with, I now know that silence that leads to a hushed wonder becomes the vehicle that takes a writer to another level. Piercing through reality leads us into a place discovered inside our willed silence—a purposeful silence of discovery like the moment outside on a macadam-topped playground on a cold January morning. "The golden sun rises/...touching snow and transforming/into frozen beams of light/ cutting through the empty/trees of the apple orchard/creating shadows that move/and whisper in the wind," wrote Katie when that moment struck her. It's not always easy to accept that moment. Jeremy entered it with these words: "Down deep my/eyes go out of focus and/I travel to my/own little world inside/my head." Then, realizing what he'd done and shaking his head to clear it, he went on: "The water around me starts to turn red/I look down and then I faint.... I wake up in a hospital."

The next two students stayed in that place perhaps because they both seemed to realize that they don't see the world quite like others do. They've accepted the fact of their difference, at least for now. David wrote, "A fantasy unfolding into its own world/sucking me into it,/mysterious capturing curiosity." Alysha traveled further than any other student of mine: "The leaves on the trees sway to an ancient/music that no human ears can hear/...but in the mist of the music/evil eyes/are on fire with hunger and greed/his angry fist desiring to close around/the music/that he cannot hear." I can only hope that all of these students stay beyond the fog and that all of them keep and treasure the ability to empty their minds and become open to the discoveries that wait just beyond the silence.

For Your Writer's Journal

Take the silence challenge. Find a spot outside. Let peace settle inside yourself. Perhaps stare at some part of the scenery that calls you to notice it. Focus on that one thing. Empty yourself of thought, logic, and any fear you might have of being judged by the "other." Expand the edges of your body, and imagine yourself spinning outward into the invisible space that surrounds you. Imagine your ears stretching out and pulling sound in like a fisherman reeling in the catch of his dreams. The leaves crackle together, speaking the language taught by the wind. Bird sounds emerge in stereo. Where are they, all these invisible singers? Voices might float up through the air. Disembodied, they seem part of nature. Now mentally describe all you see, hear, and feel with words. Logic? Let it go. Let the words flow as unbidden as the wind. When you're ready, when the moment lets you, go back inside or grab the journal you brought with you outside and spill the words onto paper. Please don't stop to think of all the rules of writing and syntax. Just let the moment be born into words. Later, read your words like you would look at a picture from a vacation.

Journaling from a Developmental Perspective

Sit quietly and, with your eyes shut, notice the bodily sensations of your muscles, bones, and internal organs, along with any auditory sensation. Describe the sensation—do not label it or categorize it. What is the sensation of a sore muscle or a strongly beating heart? For many of you, this is a first-time experience of actually feeling your body, noticing sounds, and describing sensation. This is the beginning of learning how quickly we tend to categorize or label our world, including the "different other" or people different from ourselves, according to what we have previously learned in our families, communities, and culture. How quickly, indeed unconsciously, we as human beings make explanatory decisions about our perceptions that affect not only our current understandings but also the lives of others, now and for generations to come.

Chapter Four
Beyond Reality

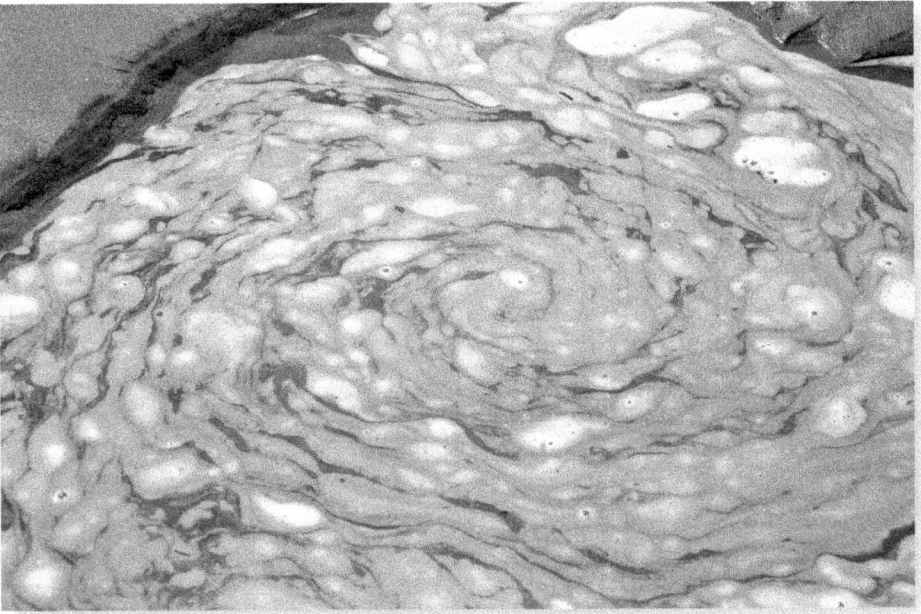

Southern Oregon Coast

From Classroom Experience

To continue exploring what is under the layer of reality, we now enter the world inside of us that eludes us except in the privacy of our dreams. Driving mindlessly through our hurried lives, we often pass it by. Yet it is here that we find out who we really are. Scary thoughts inhabit this dark place, thoughts we often feel safer leaving behind in the mists of night. There can be magic behind those mists.

Come with me through the waking world and into the place where reality is suspended and anything can happen. No, I don't expect you to fall asleep. There are ways to trick the mind into leaving the safety of the here and now. This is more than daydreaming; it is a purposeful suspension of the "now."

In the classroom, writing assignments often have as their driving force the need to explain, to use logical thought, to show the progression necessary for an essay. But poets are free to leave all of that behind. We fall into the hidden well inside ourselves and struggle to bring up to the surface the surprising water swirling in its depths. This is the realm of the unconscious mind, the beloved spaces of Freud and Jung. I explain to students that the unconscious mind is like the basement of a house where all kinds of memories are stored and forgotten.

For the school year that we are following in this book, I chose water symbols so often present in dreams. Other years, I have focused on houses and all their various rooms and parts. To create the atmosphere necessary to take an inner journey, I create a "dream machine" in the classroom. Once I have the writing materials ready and the assignment has been explained and understood, I introduce atmosphere. First, I turn out the lights. Then I start soft music. This year I choose Debussy's "La Mer." Then, as the students write, I circle around the room, weaving through rows of desks reading poetry full of water imagery. For example, I read poems by Denise Levertov, Octavio Paz, and Pablo Neruda. The students are free to grab one word from a group of words, but not a whole group. Once enough words are collected, I ask them to mix them up in any way they want to create a poem. Or they can skip the list and simply start to write.

When I ask these young writers to turn off the critic inside their heads, to just let words pop out and to not worry about making sense, the poems often surprise their writers. Sometimes the poets scare themselves. When they feel the fear of letting people inside their inner selves, I remind them that they can write the poem as though it were about someone else. They can speak in that "other voice" or create imagery about a symbol such as water that speaks to its place in our minds and hearts. With such atmosphere, the poetic focus of this lesson is easily achieved. I want the writers to show a mood and to come into the place where they can experience the symbols and their relationship to them. With this comes the possibility of birthing into being a whole new way of understanding the human condition with its emotional undercurrents.

I will never forget one student. She was in an earlier class in which we used houses and their various parts for symbolism. I want to share a part of her poem. This illustrates vividly how poetry and the imagination can be used to express hidden realities. As the music played and I read, I could see this fifth-grader getting increasingly agitated. She beckoned me over and whispered that she wanted to write about her loss of a friend. She did write about that, but into her poem crept the sense of her difference. She is a bright, introspective child and is a writer with perceptions beyond her years. The poem "Stuck" begins with a description of a friend leaving with someone new. Then it ends like this: "I still/have my friends/on the/inside./I am/stuck/in between/ two worlds,/as I always will be/stuck."

From a Development Perspective

Often, the creative portal of a poetry class allows children to enter into their own private, subconscious mental activity—the subterranean space where we work out the details of our everyday conflicted thinking while we carry on in the conscious world we cohabit with others. Here, children can use the creative act to begin to integrate—make friends with—aspects of the self that may confuse or trouble them, or they can begin to become aware of parts that cannot be tolerated as self.

From Classroom Experience

The poems that result surprise their creators as well as me. There is often a struggle to leave logic and explanations behind. But as the pencil keeps pushing across and down the page, amazing insights emerge. One student stayed inside the safety of speaking about what water does, but even so, the poem succeeded: "The magic of the waters/ is like the glimmer in the sea./And every movement deserves/its small and flowing sound." The flowing rhythm of this poem pulls the reader in and makes it hard to stop reading. The poet found the rhythm and mood of the sea.

From a Development Perspective

In all the possibility that this moment provided, it may be that her unconscious also slipped in to make a subtle statement about the magic and the importance of every movement and feeling, no matter how small. To notice and be noticed is to say yes to existence—the existence of the water and the existence of the self.

From Classroom Experience

The treasure of this lesson is that students become open to a vast new way of knowing. Here is a vivid description full of new ways of looking, metaphor, and mood: "The rain puddles on the ground like/the water in the sea sky of crystal stars/on the snow moon of night rain."

The following poem sprang out of nowhere and is amazing. Its author focused on the emotion of sadness and used water effectively to show it. The last stanza reads, "Sadness tears/bring all your fears/and clash them together./The fear and the sorrow/kill your heart/and break you deep inside."

From a Development Perspective

The poetic environment sparks a revelation of emotional intelligence, displaying an understanding and empathy for even the most difficult of human feelings. Expression of empathy for a deeply felt experience, whether personal or identified in the other, opens the student to an awareness of the interconnection that this culture, in its striving for independence, tends not to acknowledge. The following poem furthers this theme as the poet expresses an awareness of the vicissitudes of the dance of life and our interconnectedness with all being.

From Classroom Experience

The following lines are from a student who, from the first, has been able to travel into realms beyond herself: "The wood of the world's fire/swirls in an everlasting dance./Tears pour down the hunched shadowy figure/as he watches his brother/caught in the dance." Technically focused, we notice the repeated beginning sounds, alliteration, and the long vowel sounds. All of these add to the rhythm and mood.

From a Development Perspective

As the world of the poet presents itself to us, situated in our own worlds, it takes on a meaning for us. What does it mean, for example, to transform oneself personally into the brook or to watch as another gets caught in the dance of the world's fire? Be the brook, get caught up in the dance—where does it take you?

From Classroom Experience

A writer's words don't need to flow on forever. Some students can capture whole worlds of thought in a few words. Later we will meet forms of poetry that require condensed language.

The following poet never uses a spare word: "Water is like life/ Rushing through and going into new forms." When we open to the world of the unconscious, some ideas seem to flow through the air and enter several minds at once. Compare the preceding poem to the following lines written for the same lesson: "A person is a drop of water/flowing through the long rapid river/of life." But then that's not too surprising if one accepts that certain images or ideas are part of what Carl Jung refers to as the "collective unconscious."

From a Development Perspective

Carl Jung, a Swiss psychiatrist who lived into the 1950s, believed that people could experience emotional healing when they understood the ways in which their difficulties were related to archetypes, images, and symbols shared by all humanity throughout time. Here we might ask ourselves, what is this force of nature— water—and how is it related to and imaged in these poems: blank ocean of green sea, endless song of tears, rushing, puddled, a drop in a long, rapid river of life? And even more so, what is the symbol or image of water you might choose in the present moment, should you open yourself to the personal meanings of timeless archetypes found in the collective unconscious?

From Classroom Experience

We'll end our water journey with a poet who found a state of total altered consciousness and perceived things completely outside of his experience: "Mind is blank ocean of green sea./Water is stone as/fire is rock that/has the endless song of/tears hitting cold, hard floor./Wind calls to the/snowy white wolves/of the Alvalik pack/to find themselves within/ what is not there but/in the flaming soul within."

For Your Writer's Journal

The challenge is to create for ourselves moments to travel inside ourselves and find what is hidden there. You don't need to carve space out consciously. Sometimes on a walk, a tree will "speak" to you. Stare at it and see what it has to say. Or wait until twilight, play music, sit with an open journal, and write whatever words want to spin off your pen. Walk with a child, not at your pace but hers. Pay attention to the stick that seems to be a treasure to her. Crouch down beside this small explorer and watch ants trail across the dirt or discover a spider spinning a web's intricate design. Create stories together as you travel down a highway and the spinning wheels of your car thread out gold like Rumpelstiltskin's rare craft.

Journaling from a Development Perspective

Your journal takes a turn, and at once it has two faces...one toward the world and one toward the self. Think of the most meaningful geographical place you have ever visited. What resonated with you there? Describe the place, and describe your thoughts and feelings about yourself there. Notice which aspect of the landscape caught your gaze. Can you imagine this place in various seasonal cycles? Write your imaginings. Notice your own seasonal and life cycles—how do they mirror the landscape changes? Which season are you in now? How do you imagine the next season of your life?

Chapter Five
Other Cultures, Other Selves

Yurok Ceremonial Grounds, California

From Classroom Experience

If you had to choose one word to describe American society, "individualistic" would certainly be on the short list. For that reason, I feel it is important to expose students to cultures that have a different focus. No journey with the goal of growing a "self" through the use of the imagination could be considered complete without stopping and spending time inside the mindset of other societies. We don't have to leave our own country to find one. Native Americans have a rich heritage and are usually the focus of a unit in the third, fourth, or fifth grade. We'll start there and then move onto a poetic form from Japan.

Native American Worldview

In traveling inside the world of the Native American, we do not leave the realm of the unconscious mind. Dreams have a reality of their own for most Native Americans. The dream world can be as real as the one we can touch, see, smell, taste, and hear. Because I live and work in the area of California once inhabited by the Ohlone tribe, I focus on them, but I also share other tribal cultures. For most Native Americans, the natural world is equal to man. Chief Seattle is quoted often. In one of his speeches, he is reported to have said, "This we know. The earth does not belong to man; man belongs to the earth. This we know. All things are connected like the blood that unites one family. All things are connected."

In another aspect of Native American belief, the world, its people, and its habitats are all cohesive and expressed as a circle. You have only to look at the medicine wheel or the dream catcher and the pictorial symbols on petroglyphs. The four directions and the four seasons form circles. The sun and moon are circles. Close observation of nature and living in the midst of it gave the Native American a visual and daily lesson in the circular connectedness of things. Furthermore, there are four elements: earth, air, fire, and water.

All of this presents poets with another way to use the imagination to speak in code about themselves. In the Native American thought world, we find ourselves not only inside dreams and imaginings, but we find our place in the vast world of nature. From these two teachers, we can learn about ourselves and how to imagine who we are and what we want to be.

From a Development Perspective

Eco-psychology, a relatively new discipline, stresses that to be psychologically healthy human beings living in a very fast-paced culture, we must strive to find a way to create and maintain a sense of intimate involvement with nature. Native Americans honored this tenet intuitively, treating the earth with reverence and passing down anthropomorphic tales of human-like animals and animal-like humans. Now, in the face of a potentially earth-alienating structure of existence, we must again somehow realize those old, fluid boundaries between ourselves and the natural world, our rootedness in nature, and our connection to all being.

From Classroom Experience

I ask students to choose a favorite direction and a favorite element. I ask someone to name the seasons and then name them again. I ask, "What shape do they form?" Then they are ready to use these to begin a journey around the four corners of themselves: the head of the north, the arms of east and west, and the feet planted in the south. Before the students write, we brainstorm about their particulars with the directions and the elements. Most classes can associate winter and cold with the north and summer and heat with the south. East and west are much more difficult. Usually someone knows that the sun rises in the east. But the west—sometimes it feels like forever before I get someone to realize that the sun sets in the west. Each of the four directions has qualities associated with it. For example, the north represents wisdom and balance, and the south represents strength and generosity. The east represents renewal and a childlike quality, and the west represents dreams and self-discovery.

Journaling from a Development Perspective

Journaling is located differently in this chapter. Location can often determine perspective. Find a comfortable place where you can journal while changing perspective, thinking about the Native American understandings of direction. Often we can associate a direction with a season of our life. What is the significance of the directions for your life? Where do you see yourself right now? How have your previous directions influenced the direction you find yourself in right now?

From Classroom Experience

To explore the four elements, the first question I ask is "What is part of the earth?" With sadness, I listened to a child at the residential school say, "Concrete." For him that was an appropriate association. The school is surrounded by asphalt and concrete. The only living thing that is visible is the hill with rocks and bushes outside of the upper wing of the school. Water is easier. It becomes a game that can go on too long, naming all the different types of water found outdoors. I usually have to pull out the possibility of moon, stars, and birds when we come to naming things of the air. Fire becomes interesting. The more scientifically aware children name volcanoes.

All of this is on a handout students receive before they start to write. I ask them to talk about themselves, their personalities, and what they want to become using the four directions. I encourage them to let the directions and the elements speak to them. Or if they want to hide themselves more, they can write a poem about what their favorite direction and elements are using metaphor and showing something of what they know about human life. As in the dream lesson, I darken the room. This time I read Native American poetry and play a CD whose music is a single Native American flute granting its haunting melody.

This is one of those "no fail" exercises. I give the students an example using 'I am.' "I am the whispering leaves at sunset./I am the roots of the tree/reaching down to the earth's center." I tell them I'm picturing one of my favorite hills. In a class for gifted children, one girl wrote, "The west speaks to me in storm language/letting me reflect on myself./Take advantage of darkness." A boy wrote, "I am what the south is./I am joyous wonders." Then the factual hill of difficulty crept in. "Water told me to take a shower." Another wrote, "The river moves rapidly./Animals drink."

Then comes the wonder of words spilled out on paper, sharing the dreams of children living in the concrete world of the residential facility: "I am an ocean splashing on your feet./I am the red in the fire you tease./I am the soil you step on./I am what you need." Another speaks about herself: "I am the moon that shines/in the dark rivers of the night./I am the sun/that warms your heart for the next day."

These words were written by a fourth-grade girl: "Earth talks to me/in a sweet swaying-tree way." A fourth-grade boy understands his possibilities: "The west is a place of things/not known.... I grow from a stream/ to a river./...Small things can/grow to something/big and important." He understands his possibilities. A fifth-grader has the gift of creating a new way of looking at herself: "Snow is a strong figure of ice./We talk softly through the skies of winter." A boy describes the element of fire: "I am fire./Flame is my power./Heat is my courage." Then the fad of the moment creeps into a poet's life and robs her imagination. Listen: "Thunder and lightning remind me of angels/making their beds."

This last example is part of a well-crafted poem. This fourth-grade boy chose to describe each part of himself using natural symbols: "My brain is the tree/that thinks the wind./The sun is my eye/that looks down and takes care of the earth." This young man succeeds in placing all of himself in the context of the natural world.

For Your Writer's Journal

Now it's your turn. Go outside. Stand with your feet firmly planted on the earth. In silence, let the earth speak to you. Feel its dependability. Sit on a rock, a log, or just grass or dirt. Let your mind drift. What time of day is your favorite? What is your favorite season, your favorite element? Describe yourself, who you are, who you want to be using the language of the natural world. Do not fret about whether it makes sense or not. Inner sense grabs its own place and pays no attention to "shoulds" or to grammar, rules, or expectations. Roam free on the wind. Soar above the earth. Travel to the far distances of yourself. Pull it all back down to earth and live—and write your discoveries down.

Journaling from a Development Perspective

Journaling takes you to a meditative exercise here. You might begin to sit, letting the earth support your weight, imagining yourself in a very safe and beautiful place. Notice what thoughts and feelings come to mind as you contemplate the interconnectedness you are experiencing right here, right now. Notice what is around you. Close your eyes. Notice what is inside you. Can you become the breeze you feel brush against your cheek? Can you imagine being a feather floating on the breeze? Spend some time reflecting and journaling on these few precious moments and the universe that you are.

From Classroom Experience

Renga

Azalea Blossom Brookings, Oregon

I know of no better way to lead students into the ideals of coopera-tion than having them play the party game Renga from Japan. It started around the thirteenth century as a form of relaxation after a poetry contest in writing linked poems called "tanka." Renga is a series of linked verses that, for the Japanese, has fewer restrictions than other more formal poetic forms. For the American of the twenty-first century, Renga is packed with rules. Earlier Rengas often had as many as one thousand stanzas. Bashō, 1644–1694, a great Japanese poet, preferred thirty-six stanzas. Bashō observed that nature is the source for the imagery and pictures of Renga. The opening stanza was called a Hokku and required that there be a season or time of year and a description showing the surroundings or set-ting for the poem. The leftover Hokku became Haiku. For more particulars about Renga, see the suggested reading at the end of this chapter.

In my years of teaching, I've discovered that in the amount of time allotted to me, I have to keep writing assignments clear and purposeful. This is a good rule to follow for anyone working with children. We want them to grow and develop but not bore them to death in the process. I love background information, however, and have to resist the tempta-tion to give students too much detail. Japanese Renga has formal rules and charts; the writers had a guide to make sure all of the elements were in place. I have suited the "rules" for children, stretching them in some cases. My main focus is to foster cooperation and to compel students to write only about nature. The primary goal of Renga in this setting is to show beauty and to look outward at the natural world rather than inward to the I, the me.

For students who need the most help in writing, I tell them that each stanza should be three lines and should include place and season. If they need help with more details, I tell them to add an object. (Rengas usually have three-line and two-line stanzas alternating, beginning with a three-line stanza.) Next we cover the ways to link the verses. The fol-lowing are some of my suggestions:

1. Write an image suggested by the previous stanza. This can be a similar image or a contrasting one.
2. Create a shift in focus.
3. Link with words from a previous stanza by doing the following:
    a. Repeating sounds
    b. Repeating a word
    c. Playing off a word
    d. Using an association with a previous word
4. Don't use emotion words. Show emotion by imagery.
5. The third line can have a new insight.

Now comes the heart of the lesson. I divide the classroom into groups. Each group is given an opening Hokku by Bashō, each representing a different season. I provide each group with a photograph representative of the season. Just before writing time, I remind them that Renga requires the group to work together. If one person doesn't observe the form, it spoils the Renga for the whole group. Because there is waiting time as the Renga is passed around, I have each student write his or her own opening Hokku and play the game with themselves.

The resulting poems show how successful this cooperative effort is. Some writers have great difficulty keeping the "I" out. They want to return to the idea of story and self. One child wrote, "Summer river is small/I climb a tree/I jump in the river." His Renga goes on to finish the story of his day at the river. The poem is not completely unsuccessful; he does write about nature, place, and season. Others have even more difficulty: "It's a weird hot autumn day./It looks dead and pretty./Someday the rain will fall." Or consider this: "Chirping in the trees/is very, very annoying because they're going to break your ears."

The next example illustrates what happens when one writer refuses to cooperate. The rest of this group was very agitated because they felt all of their efforts were ineffective because of this one student. After using an opening Hokku by Bashō, this particular boy wrote, "It's like a calculator./It's asking me questions like what school did I go to?" The writers who followed ignored his stanza and began linking to the opening Hokku. In the end, the rest of the Renga worked.

Some students refuse to write a Renga because they want to write only in the manner of their particular cultural group. In contrast, other students who are just learning English write, and their poems have a unique quality because of the influence of their native language. One Korean immigrant wrote, "I feel so soft, beautiful and prettiest/in the world excitement, smooth and flowers/are talking to the lots of other flower/and mountain chattering/silver grass."

For most writers, this lesson is successful. Once the dreaded first word is pulled from the pencil, the words fall easily into place. A few examples follow from a Renga created by a group of three students:

Sunshine breaks
through the clouds
showering us in light. David

Mist stretching in a forest
gnarled trees bent in knots hide
in silence. Laura

On the mountain
trees are tumbling
down on summer wings. Monica

These last stanzas represent a Renga that grew out of images suddenly born from another world.

Summer rains—
leaves of the plum
cold wind color

Moving river in the sun,
spring wind, cold wind
Spring trees smell like pine

The tree's pine smell brushes in
the hot wind. The sun falls.
The forest weeps.

Winter comes as the trees
still there are bare with
weeping tears.
Saimara, Chelsea, Brian, Kimberly

Give your family, your students, a chance to foster in themselves the thoughts of another culture. Organize a Renga party game. Each person might want to write his or her own Hokku. The game can go on for days, even months. Stanzas can be added whenever an image demands to be placed on paper. There are ongoing Renga on the Internet, where you can see ongoing dialogue about Renga. Below is some suggested reading and one of many helpful web links:

1. William J. Higginson, *The Haiku Seasons: Poetry of the Natural World* (New York: Kodansha International, 1996).
2. Ron Padgett, ed., *The Teachers & Writers Handbook of Poetic Forms* (New York: Teachers & Writers Collaborative, 1987).
3. The following website refers to earlier books by William J. Higginson and features examples of Renga and discussions by various people: www.ahapoetry.com/renga.htm

Chapter Six
The Empathy Wilderness

Florence, Italy

❦

From Classroom Experience

Traveling through other cultures often seems easier than creating a sympathetic view of someone other than you. Sometimes it appears that poets, more than other types of writers, are concerned with the self. Delving into yourself is important, but I believe that the other people who inhabit our world should command our focus as well.

From a Development Perspective

That which is different always makes us stop, notice, and explain so that we can make sense of the unfamiliar. Why we stop there becomes the real question. It is in the act of explanation that we often do the most destructive disservice. Explanation amounts to an action of assimilation. We make sense of the "different other" with the information we already have on hand, the schemata we function with that allow us ease in getting through life. It is only when we allow for "dis-ease," when we do not rush to explain, when we sit with the difference and wonder at it, that we then open ourselves to the possibility of surpassing explanation and embracing true understanding. The key here is staying open even when it is out of our comfort zone. The path involves giving up our preconceptions, our worn-out ways of making sense of our world, staying vulnerable, and finally, in that vulnerability, accommodating to something new. The demand is that we must give up part of who we are to grow into that which we will become.

From Classroom Experience

"The pain of becoming" became evident in a session with fourth- and fifth-grade gifted students. I walked around the classroom slowly, holding a picture of a portly gentleman in a vest, trousers, and hat. His gray hair was wild and longer than what was normal for the first decades of the twentieth century. He looked relaxed, with his hands in his pockets. The picture was in profile, and the man stood with a warm expression on his face and his head tipped up to the sun like some benign carved figure on the prow of a ship. As I circled through the tables, I asked what the students could tell about this man from his picture. The first answer was "He's fat!" My response? "Would you like to have someone say that about you? What can you tell about this man from his face and posture? Look at the expression on his face. How do you suppose he's feeling?" Response from students: "Who cares? He's fat."

Finally one student came up with this observation: "He looks like he's wondering about what's in the sky." Excellent! The picture is of Albert Einstein.

From a Development Perspective

Although its roots are innate, empathy is a learned behavior. We can help students develop this skill by asking them to think about alternate ways to interpret something or someone they are observing. This requires that they temporarily step outside of their current schemata as they forage around for new ways to understand the reality of the other in front of them. They must know at the outset that they can understand the other without becoming the other. They do not need to lose themselves in the other to empathize; they can "cross over" and return to themselves. They must know, however, that this interpersonal perspective-taking will change them. They will not only know the other in a new way, but they will have begun gaining access to a possible new intersubjective process of seeing and being seen, of knowing and being known. This will only serve to help them strengthen and deepen their understanding of the concept of interconnectedness to all being. The next exercise promotes this foraging for new understandings.

From Classroom Experience

For the students in the school year being tracked in this book, I introduced empathy as the target of a lesson using the art of Edward Hopper, an American artist who lived from 1882 until 1967. His scenes, all set in America and from his own individual point of view, are spare with vivid colors. He tends to show people in a solitary state or houses all by themselves—even empty streets find meaning for him. Not only does this lesson require empathy; it also demands that the students put themselves into scenes from another era and into the lives of people unfamiliar to them.

To stretch students to reach into the lives of people completely unfamiliar to them, I ask them to imagine themselves in the picture. They can actually become the person in the picture. After doing that, I ask them to imagine what they are feeling, why they are in this particular place.

Because Hopper often paints pictures with no people, we discuss the symbolism inherent in houses. If the house appears empty, it is natural for some students to guess that it can show loneliness, even fear. If the house seems inhabited, it can show comfort. I encourage the students to place themselves inside the house.

Not surprisingly, a few students don't even try to go inside the picture, let alone empathize with the people in it. Why imagine a life outside of one's own? "No point," they announce. Or they toss out a poem with no deep thought. "I am very rich./I own the whole block." Another student could find no images, no unusual ideas. He struggled with behaving. His folder was cluttered and in disarray.

Then there are the students who are blocked before they start. They say, "I can't do this" or "I can't see anything." Just about the time I wonder if this attempt at empathy is doomed to complete failure, I see a line like "Sitting in the compartment/waiting in bewilderment/the heavy cushion comforts my sorrow." Another image leaps off the page: "I walk into/ the lobby/everybody's eyes/are on me." Yes! This student has begun the treasure hunt of looking for what isn't there, for possibilities of thought processes in the pictured people. In short, the task is to imagine the experience of their lives—empathy.

As the year moved on, other gems emerged from writers. Students who had been exploring the world of the imagination for two years grabbed onto this lesson and expressed a depth of understanding that illustrates the power of going inside the "other" outside of one's self. Consider this poem from Lauren: "Houses, alone, empty.../I look into silver gray slits of eyes./Shadows of the hills/of the houses loom/over the empty faces of the observers, over me." Lauren discovered a new way of looking at the world around her—the "surprise" moment that is the goal of all poetry. Poetry should leave its reader with the thought, "I've never seen it that way before." As we develop into our full potential, we should all prowl the terrain of our lives waiting for those surprises that grab us out of the ordinary and ease us into the world of the unknown.

Another student who the year before was constantly wadding up his poems and tossing them to the floor rather than rewrite began to blossom and accept that his "creative" spelling did not mean he was not a good writer with important perceptions waiting to be born into the world. This boy was brilliant, yet his brain refused to spell in a correct fashion. But his words can be understood. He ended his poem titled "Finding Company" written to the picture *Cape Cod Evening* by Hopper with these words: "The dog *comse* forth/but I don't *firiten* (frighten) it/because in/this *werld/ eny* company/ is perfect/company." This ending was perfect for the world depicted by Hopper.

The following lines are from a poem judged by its poet to be a complete failure. I reminded her that this feeling often comes when the poem takes control and the poet is left wondering where the words came from. Listen: "Her life slips by like water through cupped hands/like the images that fly past the train-seat window." And that's only the beginning. Another girl, Charlotte, crawls inside an imagined scene with a woman completely out of her own experience. She writes, "As I leave she turns/

around, smiles softly/without a sound./Reading her book/the widow weeps/under the sun that/burns her." These writers have succeeded in their attempts to journey into the wilderness of empathy.

Another successful journey comes from Theresa, a student I thought I'd lost. She had been an outstanding writer the year before, but this year she was tossing out words in sloppy handwriting with no attempt at excellence. Then she wrote this: "She does not dare to move/as she sits there/for the words are/flowing from the/page through her/mind to her heart." From that lesson on, Theresa wrote up to her usual high standards.

For Your Writer's Journal

There are many ways to journey into empathy with a child or by yourself. In the car as you pass people, guess what they're doing and feeling. Sit in a crowded public place and watch the play before your eyes, an improvisational one that supplies stories for you to create. What is that teenage girl feeling as she walks by tossing her hair back, swinging packages full of clothes purchased to create an image of herself that is a work in progress? Or become the young man who so carefully parks his motorcycle, cradles his helmet, and nervously leaves the bike behind. Imagine the bravery required to leave so expensive a machine parked in front of a mall. Imagine the mother waiting for his safe arrival home. Magazines and newspapers are full of pictures of real people. Look at them in isolation from the words around them. You can even cut them out, as I do, for lessons. Let your child create stories or a poem around the face or faces in the picture.

Journaling from a Development Perspective

Journaling about your experiences of practicing "getting to know" or "seeing" will teach you much about yourself as well as the "other." What draws you to another, and what makes you want to keep your distance? How do contexts vary? What do you understand of them, and what is mystery? Can you develop an understanding of what it means to describe as opposed to interpret? Can you describe what you see purely? Can you allow yourself to wonder and develop many interpretations on a theme? Can you question your interpretations and where they come from inside you? How does your context of self and your world inform your construct of the "other"? Can you imagine the other "seeing" you, "getting to know" you? What do you think they might see as the "other" works to "cross over" to you? What of their experiences in the world might directly influence their "knowing" of you? What could be some variations on your answer to this?

So a mind grows and reaches out to realms beyond it. This is part of our necessary work as developing people. We must place ourselves in the hearts and minds of those around us and find their invisible pain and thoughts. Even happiness must be traced because if we don't know what makes people happy, how can we create moments to bring joy to their lives? I've often had the experience of being with someone who remarks, "I'm really in pain." I look at them and know their pain must be real. I can see it in their fidgeting, in their struggles to get comfortable, in the frowns that cloud their faces. And yet I cannot *see* the pain. There is so much of the human condition that is impossible for us to perceive. Yet if we don't succeed in crossing the barrier of invisibility, we can never truly share with each other.

Chapter Seven
Exploring Your Geo-Center

Sonoma Coast, California

From Classroom Experience

No journey of the imagination would be complete without exploring your inner landscape, or "geo-center". Whether it's on a conscious level or not, each of us has been influenced by the geography of the place where we grew up. Take a moment and think about what types of places make you feel at home. I grew up on a citrus ranch located on the edge of a small canyon in southern California. It was a space of granite rocks, eucalyptus, and seasonal flowing water that fell over the granite into a pool that was there all year 'round. Shaded by trees, towering rock walls, and shrubs kept green by the water, the canyon—my canyon—was a cool place in the summer and a world full of endless places to explore. In the canyon, I was a cowboy guarding my hoard of rocks. When the occasional hunter passed through, I curled up in a dark cave to protect my rocks and myself from the guns. In my imagination, I was the Lone Ranger out to keep the West safe. Even now, the feel of cool rock gives me a sense of peace and security, and the smell of blossoming orange trees and the distinctive odor of eucalyptus fill my mind with the word "home."

Because I am so aware of the place of importance that this canyon sphere has in my life, I try to help students find out where their geo-center is. I've discovered that, among the children I work with, most are not completely aware of the variety of geography around them. They know we live in a valley bordered by hills, but the bay to the west of us hides from their conscious minds, even though it's a scant ten minutes away. Their lives are more bounded by the boulevard that goes through town and the streets they travel on. Fortunately, they recognize and know the names of redwood and oak.

From a Development Perspective

The experience of a sense of grounded, sacred space is much like the experience of feeling complete and resting in that completeness. It is that place, when you close your eyes, you can experience with all your senses. It comes alive for you, and you also come alive in that moment. The larger question here is, are our children exposed to experiencing with all of their senses in spaces that are non-threatening, non-electronic (the word "natural" comes to mind), and non-intrusive? Can our children create visions in their minds of places that give them a sense of whole-ness? Can they learn to become aware of these places with all of their senses so that when they cannot be there, when they cannot experience safety, groundedness, and sacredness firsthand, they can close their eyes and be there in an imaginary moment?

From Classroom Experience

Whenever I do a ten session residency, I approach this idea of the importance of place in our lives. Which approach I take depends on the cycle of lessons. The lesson I like the best uses model poems by the Chilean poet Pablo Neruda. His work is infused with the landscape of Chile and his home by the sea. I trade off using different poems. My favorites are "The Stones of Chile," "The Night in Isla Negra," and "I Will Return."

It is difficult to challenge a group of fourth- and fifth-graders with the concept of the "spirit" of a place—that indefinable air that each place has. If you've been to New York, it is hard to miss the frenetic energy of that city. In contrast, an ancient redwood grove fills the visitor with a spiritual feeling and the sense that there must be something powerful outside of what we see. Desert spaces leave us feeling small and lost, as do large canyons. While I was doing graduate work at Mills College in Oakland, California, I took an interdisciplinary class on the environment and American literature. I presented a research paper on the shaping influence of geography on our perceptions of the world. People from the Midwest, used to the reaching, flat plains, felt trapped and hemmed in by the twin boundaries of mountains and ocean in California. But for Californians, these geographical boundaries called forth the freedom to explore the many different types of landscape found in the state and the ocean that provides its western boundary.

To help my workshop students grapple with this concept of place, we first talk about observation skills that writers of all types, including poets, must have. I ask students to describe for me what it means to look at something closely. Many people have never stopped to look closely, and when they are asked what they see, they respond, "Nothing." I then introduce the concept of "mindful looking." This is very simply the idea of going through your day paying close attention to small details. Even if you aren't a writer, "mindful looking" adds dimension to your life. It gives the place where you happen to be a greater reality. It is at this point that we discuss the geography of where we live. Next I ask people to remember outdoor places they love being in. When the concept begins to sink in, I ask them how the landscape around us shapes our attitudes and our moods.

To arrive at a poem, I take the class outside. At each school, I try to find a spot with a view, dirt or grass, and trees or shrubs. I ask the students to sit quietly by themselves and to pay close attention to what they see and hear. They are free to imagine themselves in another place that they particularly enjoy. I ask them to think about how where you are affects your mood. We talk about the difference between busy cities with their frantic pace and the quieter rhythm of suburbs, for example.

By this time, we have discussed the boundaries of the valley we live in, and most are aware now and reminded of the ocean to our west. The challenge, of course, is to trap all of this into a poem so that a reader can sense the mood and the spirit of what the poet is describing.

But the biggest challenge is get the students to sit quietly. Outside? All right! Let's play. Let's goof off. Some classes manage the quiet challenge very well. Others don't. But even in the midst of group chaos, there are a few who do go sit quietly by themselves. Those are the writers who succeed in journeying into the world of inner geography.

Here are some lines from students who were able to travel inside the geo-space that they live in. Ryan G. wrote, "I live in a valley with/Mile-long hills and shrubs.../yellow rays/Shine down through the clouds/...like a never-ending light year/Running through the hills." Giving her poem the title "Where I Live," Elizabeth L. wrote, "...there's an ocean in the sky with white/fluffy foam./Many trees breathe./Clouds move together like they're on a field trip." Junn C. titled his poem "Living in a Valley." He wrote, "It is like living in a crater with trees and structures."

But this lesson came post-September 11, 2001, so some of the poems, while dealing with place, crept into a dark world that surprised their writers. When John C. stopped writing, it was like he was waking from a dream. His poem, titled "The End of All," contained lines like this: "The black clouds of death swarm/through the air.... It's not hot like it should be/but suspiciously cold." John B. wrote as well about the struggle between darkness and light. In his case, the light wins. These are a few lines that illustrate the contrasts found in his poem: "Light hits the/leaves./Then it goes./The earth turns black./Everything is cold./The sun fights for / freedom./With a devastating blow,/The sun knocks the/Coldness away...."

Come with me now into spring and into a school where I've been teaching for more than ten years. This school is situated on a hill from which you can see something of the shape of the valley. When the wind blows the fog and clouds away, you can see the San Francisco Bay shining in the distance. To the north, the school is bounded by open land owned by the water district. There we can see the hills without the intrusion of homes. The new green grass waves in a soft wind, and oats, eucalyptus, and pines dot the hills as they flow wave-like away from us. All of this becomes a near-perfect backdrop for writing poetry.

As always, I start by asking each class what the word "geography" means. Fresh from making relief maps of California, their answers are typical of every school. Geography, to them, is maps, the study of land, or the study of other countries. Now the online *American Heritage Dictionary of the English Language* comes to the rescue. "Geography—1. The study of the earth and its features and of the distribution of life on the earth, including human life and the effects of human activity. 2. The physical characteristics, especially the surface features, of an area. 3. A book on geography."[5] The following is a list of the questions I used to start the students thinking about place:

1. How does the geography of where we live shape our attitudes and our moods?
2. Do we always think about the landscape around us or look at it closely?
3. What are the characteristics of the land here in our city?
4. What borders our city?
5. How does having these choices of landscape affect us?
6. How would it be different for you if you lived in a desert? Or right by the ocean?

In answering the question about attitude and mood, the most common response was that living in a cold climate would be depressing. None of the students felt that they paid attention to the land around them. All of the classes knew that our town is full of hills and grass. Surprisingly, only one class knew it was a valley. When asked to describe a valley, they answered that a valley is a flat place. I broadened that concept by asking them to imagine that a valley is like the bottom of a bowl. The sides of the bowl become the hills or mountains that border a valley. These classes were good at naming the plants that grow around us. Their answers listed willows, oaks, redwoods, and weeds. Several mentioned the lake that is here. I explained that it isn't a natural lake; it is a reservoir. What was dammed up to create it? Again, someone in each class knew that a stream or creek had been dammed up to create a nearby lake. All of the classes knew that to the west there is an ocean. Obviously, the location of this school was a large factor in the ability of these classes to describe their surroundings accurately.

It is time to explore the product produced by these classes. For me, that is both the fun and the source of possible dismay. "Have I really succeeded?" is the question always at the back of my mind as I leave a school. I'm going to look first at the fourth- and fifth-grade combination class. Several of the students simply observed what they saw with

---

[5] *The American Heritage Dictionary* (Houghton Mifflin Harcourt Publishing Company, 2011,2012)

lines like "Birds soar through the sky." Another observed, "Green grass/ on the ground/Sun out today." These lines do not equal failure in that the poets did write exactly what they saw, but they do not go into the deeper task of describing the "spirit" of place. Other students in the class, including Hawly H., wrote at a deeper level: "Open a door/to a whole new world/...Tall trees/lock you in./...This is such a peaceful world." This is from Ethan J: "Where I live it is always happy/...and nights are always calm/and I sleep well in my valley." Camille K. conveys her feelings with her word pictures: "Luscious green grass spreads across/an open field/... hills around me/trees spread across them/...a valley/a huge valley."

The next quotes come from the two fifth-grade classes. Jane G. chose to simply describe the effect of buildings being built on the hills, but in doing that, she went into the heart of how building changes our spaces: "Round hills almost have nothing but trees and/ flowers....Kids/run around with joy. But houses pop up/and ruin the children's joy." Robert T. captured the feel of being by the ocean with these lines: "As I watch by the soothing ocean/my eyes are hypnotized by a/soothing song that rows back/and forth while my eyes turn/aqua blue." As is often the case, several students simply conveyed word pictures with lines like, "I see the/ clouds. They go/as slow as a/turtle...." Another poem, by Jacqueline E., has the following stunning images: "Black as coal,/the bird/glistens/in the melting sun./...You hear chirps/...in the draping trees/on the dusty ground." Another student goes into what she perceives as the spirit of this valley we call home. Amanda M. calls her poem "In the Valley": "Grassy hills out/in the distance..../The trees reach/up into the sky/...Mysterious voices/come through/ the clouds/birds chase/after each other/as it was/ before here/in the valley." This student goes under what is normally perceived as a whole new way of looking. From Michelle G.: "All around me/the flat and dirt-covered land/stretches everywhere/...trying to reach something/...the land will never get/Or maybe it's trying to/fly away/from a deep-hearted memory/to never end/to never change."

It is difficult to know if a lesson like this creates a felt change. I feel encouraged when I read comments on the evaluations that students fill out at the end of the workshops. Some of their comments tell me that, for at least some students, perceptions have changed. They carry the feelings discovered in writing about the "spirit" of place into how they perceive themselves as writers. Here are two examples of their comments: "When I write, I see farther." "When I write, I feel like a river that can't be stopped."

For Your Writer's Journal

The next time you are outside, try to see farther than you have before. When you travel, look around you and try to sense how this different environment shapes the people who live there. Participate in the life of a place so that you can feel, for a small amount of time, that you are a part of the life you find there. Be the river that can't be stopped, and flow into new spaces of our world.

Journaling from a Development Perspective

In journaling about your geo-center, think of when you felt most at home, most grounded. What were the essential features that connected you to that sacred space? Let your mind wander to experiences you may have had in this space. Describe them. Describe how you felt. Were significant others around? (Note: If there are times in your life when you are experiencing physical pain, try going to your sacred space, imagining it with all of your senses, breathing it in, and resting in that body-based image. You may find that you can experience pain-free or pain-lessened moments.)

For further reading, here are some books I have enjoyed:

1. Brian Leigh Molyneaux, *The Sacred Earth* (Alexandria, Virginia: Time-Life Books, 1995).
2. Linnie Marsh Wolfe, ed., *John of the Mountains: The Unpublished Journals of John Muir* (Madison, Wisconsin: The University of Wisconsin Press, 1979).
3. Ann Haymond Zwinger, *The Mysterious Lands* (New York: Truman Talley Books/Plume, 1990).
   A good resource for books about the natural world is www.longitude books.com.

Chapter Eight
The Arrival Point: The Thinking Self

Oregon Coast

❦

From Classroom Experience

Every journey has a destination. This journey of the imagination doesn't set out looking for a place you can touch and see. It attempts to climb the mountain of the mind, to cross the ocean of thought, and to flow with a river called "freedom." Why freedom? Because only a mind that is free from the norms of thought can come up with the new ideas, the surprises that make poetry a joy to read. It is this same free mind that bounds into scientific discovery and imagines what previously was unimaginable.

In poetry, the word "freedom" can also suggest feeling free enough to experiment with form. Each writer tends to have a style that is his or hers alone—a comfortable place, a poetic home. I'm thinking of one student whose first really outstanding poem was in two-line stanzas. In commenting on his poem, I noted that this was his best poem yet. For the rest of our time together, every poem had two-line stanzas. That form became his comfort zone.

From a Development Perspective

By the time you may be working with children, they may have gone through several crises of psychosocial development (see the Introduction).

If they are able to navigate these stages successfully, they will have the capacity to have a bodily sense of trust in the world and to move around in the world with confidence in their capacity to do so. They will be able to step out with initiative and the will to have the drive and energy to accomplish tasks. They will, if they are in adolescence, be struggling with the great question of personal identity and who they are in relation to the rest of the world.

However, if they have had difficulty in one or more of these stages, the outcome might be quite different. For example, they may have very little trust in the world, in others, and even in their own capacities. They may doubt their own ability to manage themselves in the world by themselves. They may demonstrate a great deal of hesitancy to try new things. They may exhibit a sense of inferiority, and if they are in adolescence, they may suffer a great deal of confusion about who they are, what they value, and who they can relate to successfully. Please know that while you may not be able to undo developmental scarring, you can help the healing process by recognizing the child where he is and understanding what needs to be encouraged for psychosocial growth. Remember that while crises get resolved at various ages, the resolution is always malleable in terms of experiences of trust, respect, recognition, encouragement, and positive acknowledgment of who they are in the moment. This is your opportunity to make a difference.

From Classroom Experience

We have arrived at the crossroads of the imagination. There are two paths. One offers safety, the other promises adventure and risk. As imagination and creativity develop, a poet reaches the place where risk taking is fun. Poets can leave behind the part of themselves that always writes in a certain style and about a particular piece of life. The mind becomes open to any image that arrives unannounced and perhaps is frightening in its lack of normalcy. How do you get students to give up structure and the safety of thinking like everyone else? How do we get rid of the phrase "We've always done it that way"?

Journaling from a Development Perspective

Journaling now takes us back in time to our personal history of the resolution of developmental crises: trust vs. mistrust; autonomy vs. doubt, initiative vs. inadequacy, industry vs. inferiority, and identity vs. confusion. Try to imagine yourself from birth to age one; ages one to two; three to six; six to twelve; and during your teen years. Take each period and think about the corresponding tasks at hand. What do you know from your memory or from the stories you have been told? What was the context of your life like at that developmental moment? How did you resolve the crises? What would you like to revisit? You can provide the same experiences of trust, respect, recognition, encouragement, and positive acknowledgment for yourself as you might for the children you serve. Write a series of affirmations that are unique to your developmental life. Recreate these on cards that you can carry with you and read through whenever you find yourself with a few minutes to yourself. You can re-vision and rewrite yourself.

For Your Writer's Journal

When thinking about change in relationship to creativity, ask yourself some questions: How do you feel when you are asked to do an old task in a completely new and unfamiliar way or when you are challenged to explore your writing skills in ways unfamiliar to you? Do you want to stay in your safe zone, or are you willing to take risks? Journal about change and its place in your life. What imagery can you find for change? Try to imagine how it would feel to have your life totally turned upside down by an outside event. How could you use your writing to transform your experience? Or look back at one of your journal entries and rewrite it from another perspective. If your entries are written in prose, re-imagine them as poetry by adding comparisons and word pictures to show your feelings. If you've written poems, pick one to rewrite, and change its form entirely. Try leaving out capitalization and punctuation. Change the poem's placement on the page. Recreate it in a set form if it is in free verse. Finally, to complete your explorations of change, journal about how it felt to break from your comfortable style of writing and thinking.

Chapter Nine
Mind Shifts: Student Experience

Perfume factory, Italy

From Classroom Experience

What happens to students who've traveled through "the door like broken wings"? Are they altered in how they perceive themselves? Does writing create a shift in their thinking? The only way to really know is to ask them. When students fill out evaluations at the end of each residency, one of the questions is "How do you feel when you write poetry?"

The quotes that follow were taken directly from student evaluations.

- When I write, I think out of the real world. I open my mind.
- I think of it (writing) as a song.
- I use my emotions and let my imagination flow.
- I feel like I am flying.
- I open up to the world. My mind lets go.
- Poetry makes you drift in your mind.
- When I write, I shut off all other ideas and thoughts. I let my mind loose.
- When I write, my mind runs wild.
- Poetry is like a flower blooming.
- I feel like I'm wandering off to another world.
- When I write, I feel great about myself.
- I let my mind do whatever it wants. My poetry is very mysterious because my mind is mysterious, too.
- Poetry is good for the soul because you let your feelings out on paper.
- When I write, I get poetry from my unconscious mind. I just write whatever comes to me. My poetry is very creative. My poetry comes from my heart and my soul.
- You discover what kind of poet you are. Some of my poetry is about dark events, tragedy, and confusion.
- When I write, I feel like I am in space.

Reading these quotes, I knew the students were on the journey with me. If all I do as a poet–teacher is help minds fly into new thoughts, then I believe all the time spent is worthwhile. So try the journey yourself. Even if you travel alone, you will discover surprises around every bend, through every poetic country. Parents, share moments of surprise and wonder with your children. If your children are too young to write, write their words for them. Let them tell you their story or poem as you capture their words on paper. A warning: This journey never ends. It carries you forward for your entire life. Writers don't need to search for the mythical fountain of youth. They have it with them inside, and its words of water flow from pens, pencils, and keyboards.

SECTION II-PRACTICAL APPLICATION IN THE CLASSROOM

Chapter Ten
How to Introduce Writing Poetry

Sorrento, Italy

Reassure students that there is no way to be wrong as long as they write. Remind them that anyone can be a poet. Each individual has her own way of writing that is unique to her. Ask her to send the "I can't do this" voice out of the room.

Depending on your class, you can start out by asking your students what poetry is for them. One answer is sure to be that poetry rhymes. In response, help students understand that while poetry *can* rhyme, it does not have to rhyme.

Why am I asking you to stress this concept? I prefer to focus on free verse when teaching children. I discourage rhyming when introducing poetry and creative thought, and I encourage, instead, the use of free verse. Rhyming is a difficult craft. It is a rare student who has a good enough command of our language to rhyme well. What happens most often is that the rhyme forces a use of words that don't fit the meaning, that create tortured syntax, or that are completely predictable.

Even free verse has its own stylistic conventions that are quite different from prose; consequently, when teaching poetry, there are specific tools to teach.

A Beginning Definition of Poetry for Students

Poetry is an art form. Like visual art, it creates pictures, but poetry uses "word" pictures so detailed that readers can see them in their minds. Like music, poetry contains sound and rhythm, which are created by line breaks and the sounds of the letters that make up the words. Line breaks give the poem a shape, almost like a sculpture. Poetry creates its own world and lets the reader in without explanations. Like all good art, poetry appeals to the feelings and creates emotions in the reader.

The Importance of Line Breaks in Free Verse

Visually, line breaks separate poetry from prose. To our ears, they create rhythm. They also create a shape the reader sees and reacts to. From the moment a reader sees a poem, he develops an impression based on the poem's shape. Greeted with regular stanzas and lines of similar length, a reader expects a more formal approach. When lines sprawl across a page and begin in various places on the page, a sense of the unexpected is there even before the poem is read.

Poetry Warm-Ups

Image Stretches: Or Extending the Image

This exercise is concrete and grounded in grammar and may require a little whining on your part. By "image," I mean a picture with words, or word picture, using specific sensory detail. I often use the phrase "word picture" instead of "image" or "simile" because it conveys what I want in a simpler fashion. I choose something to look at that is in the room. To start off, I make my choice—in this case "window"—and ask the question "Does 'window' all by itself create a detailed word picture in your reader's mind?" If someone says yes, ask if anyone disagrees with that. Explain that "window" by itself doesn't show a specific window in a certain place but only conveys windows in general. It is time for more questions. Can someone suggest something we can add to the word "window" to make us see a specific window? The answers start coming. As words are suggested, I add them to a sentence. Typically, the answers start off with "clear," "square," and "can see outside." Rarely do the students think to put the window in a wall in a room that gives me a chance to whine, "But the window is just hanging in space. Where is this window? I can't see it." (This is really quite fun—whining with a purpose.) I whine, I complain, I drag out details until the window has a room, a wall that we can see, and something visible through the window that's described in detail. I ask for adjectives—color, shape, size. I ask for comparisons. What does the window remind you of that isn't a window? I usually ask for descriptive verbs to replace the boring "is" and "are." These, in turn, beg for more details. "The large, square window is in the living room" gets replaced with "The large, square window in the cold and empty living room forces me to look out at the leafless trees that grow along the dead lawn. Through the clear window, I see a shadowy figure walking slowly through the trees." Descriptive verbs not only add interest but can suggest a mood that can lead to more details. By the time we're done, we have a paragraph describing a specific window, and we've snuck in using adjectives and verbs correctly in a sentence. Not only that, but we're well on our way to a poem or a story.

At this point, if you're only introducing writing poetry, you could choose to add line breaks to your expanded description. You could even make it longer if the class seems really into it. Suggest putting line breaks in a place that creates surprise and makes the reader wait to see what's coming. Here's how the description above could become a poem with just the addition of line breaks:

The large, square window
in the cold and empty living room
forces me to look out at the leafless
trees that grow along the dead lawn.
Through the clear window, I see a shadowy
figure walking slowly through the trees.

To extend the concept of line breaks, the class could play with putting the breaks in different places, either to create surprise or because a different length of line might be interesting. Let your imagination go, and encourage your students to do the same. It's amazing what you can do to the mood and feel of a poem with just a few changes. When I change the voice of the poem to an impersonal description, the mood changes. Whatever you change, the changes in line and voice make it tempting to add a few more lines.

A large, square window
in a cold and empty living room
looks out at the leafless
trees that grow along the dead lawn.
Through its clear glass, a shadowy
figure appears walking
slowly through the trees.

A word of caution: Always remind students that any images, sentences, or ideas that come up in group warm-up and practice are not available for use in their work. It is tempting for someone who's stuck to use the class's examples.

Poetry Ball *(Repeated from Chapter Two)*

Poetry Ball is a ball game with words. Before I toss out the first word "ball," I tell students that the object of this game is to come up with two completely unrelated words and create a comparison from them. I pick the first word by using an object in the room so that there is something visual to begin with. Many times, I'll start with the word "desk." "Desk" becomes the first ball. To "catch" the ball and create their own word ball, students have to let a word pop into their heads, whether it makes sense or not. I encourage them to say the first word that comes to them. When they have a word, I tell them to raise their hands. When enough hands are raised to make it fun, I choose a student. It often happens at this point that the first word that pops out is really quite logical. So for now, "table" is the new ball. I point out that this is really a lot like a desk, so we need something wilder. Now the students must bounce off the word "table." It may take a few words for the connections to stop being logical. But sooner or later, the answers will get wild. One boy came up with the word "grass." When I get an answer like that, I stop quickly because I know we have the potential for a simile they can all visualize.

To end the game, they have to take two of the words and make a comparison, an unusual connection, using them. We'll use "desk" and "grass" to illustrate. You have to do something to both "desk" and "grass" to make them equal. So my question is, what do grass and a desk have in common? Puzzled frowns may greet this question. It's time for another question. What do you do at a desk? Someone may say "study." I push some more. What else do you do with a desk? Sit? Knowing I need more to get an image, I'll ask more questions. Can you sit on grass? What kinds of activities would involve sitting on grass? On this day, one answer was "picnic." At last, we had a shot at a great comparison.

At this point, I ask students to come up with a sentence comparing a desk to grass using the idea of a picnic. Obviously there is no one correct answer. "When I sit at my desk and study, it's like having a picnic for the mind" pops into my head, so I know I have an answer if they don't come up with one. Here's theirs: "Sitting at your desk at school and learning is like having a picnic on the grass at the park."

Chapter Eleven
Metaphor and Simile—Looking at the Ordinary in a New Way

Sorrento, Italy

❧

Metaphors and similes have been called "the heart of poetry" because they allow the poet to create the new way of looking that makes a poem work. No journey into the world of poetry would be complete without them. If the reader gets to the end of a poem and doesn't feel as though she has discovered something new, then the poem probably hasn't succeeded. Metaphors and similes, or comparisons for simplicity's sake, allow the poet to put two completely different things together to create a whole new way of looking at ourselves or our world. Comparisons make unusual connections. They let our minds leap from one thing to the next like we do in Poetry Ball. Comparisons are not some mystical creative tool that is hard to use. Young children use them constantly. Clouds look like bears. Logs look like dragons, and chicken feed falling from a hand becomes snow. To help students understand, I call comparisons "the math of poetry." Below are definitions and some poetry math.

Lesson Preparation
1. Either have copies of the model poem for each student or have it written where each student can see it.
2. Have some music ready to play during writing time.

Explaining Metaphor and Simile
Metaphor:
- Metaphor uses "is" or "of."
- It makes the comparison appear to be true.

Simile:
- Simile uses "like" or "as" to make the comparison.

Poetry Math: Metaphor and Simile
1. Both metaphors and similies use an equation that makes one thing equal to another completely different thing.
2. This equation creates a picture the reader can see. On the board, write "Metaphor—Is." Under it with some space left, write "Simile—Like." In the middle, put an = sign, leaving room for the nouns the students decide to use.

How to use the equation:

1. The = sign is represented by the words "like" "as," or "is," "of." (This makes it true.)
2. Do a brief round of Poetry Ball. Tell students to raise their hands when they have an object to suggest for the first word. Keep the word ball going until you have at least four words. Pick two that you think will work to illustrate how to create a comparison. Two favorites in classrooms have been the words "clock" and "eye."
3. Show students that the = sign is "is or of" in a metaphor and "like or as" in a simile. After they understand it, have them create a metaphor and a simile using "clock" and "eye," making sure they create a word picture with at least a few details. Here's how the equation looked when we were done:

Metaphor - Is

Clock=Eye

Simile-like

Metaphor: The round clock *is a large eye* watching us work as it ticks off the time with its unequal arms.

Simile: The round clock *is like a large eye* watching us work as it ticks off the time with its unequal arms.

Presenting the Model Poem—Word Pictures of an Ordinary Moment

Finding the Model Poem

For each lesson, I tell where you can find the model poem on the web. We are unable to print the poems in this book because doing so would be a violation of copyright law. There is always the option of using a poem you already have and enjoy. Using poetry you like yourself is very important for your ability to convey both its meaning and its craft. If you use a poem that I haven't listed, you will need to change the focus of your brainstorming and your assignment so that they both fit your model.

Introduction

The world of poetry is fascinating because it bursts with limitless possibilities. One of the most important aspects of poetry is its ability to look at perfectly ordinary moments and show them in unexpected and new ways. The following suggested poems focus on different things. One uses an ordinary moment. The other poem is created using the importance of dreaming about the future. They both contain clear metaphors for students to discover.

Suggested Model Poems

You can find model poems at www.poets.org.

When you get to the site, click on "Poets and Poems." Type in the name of the poet you want or the title and click on "Search." The suggested poem for this lesson is "Dreams" by Langston Hughes.

This poem is short and very accessible for students. The use of metaphor is clear and easy to spot. Hughes uses short lines and is very sparse with words. Note the short stanzas as well. By choosing this form for his poem, he forces the reader to focus quickly on the message the poem conveys. Because poetry is music with words, Hughes uses a repeated line to begin each stanza like a short refrain in a song. Each stanza ends with what is important to Hughes: what happens when dreams die. Remind students if you wish that as a black man in the middle of the twentieth century, Langston Hughes had to struggle to reach his dreams, but he did succeed. When going through the poem with students, ask them first what do they think it means. Then see if anyone can find the metaphors. What does the poem show the students about the importance of dreams? Did it help them to see loss of hope in a new way?

"A Happy Birthday" by Ted Kooser is another short poem with one sharp, clear metaphor at the end. This poem takes a simple moment and turns it into both a painting and a gift. You can see the light fading, and then you realize that the poet has taken a simple time and invested it with meaning. He has looked at each small detail and made it important. This is another sparse poem with no wasted words. Make sure your students are clear about what the poem is showing. Lead them to the second line, which shows how a line break can lead the reader on. The clearest metaphor is in the last line. Notice with them the surprise with which metaphor allows the poem to end. Yet there is one metaphor hidden. See if anyone can find it. In the fifth line, Kooser makes the reader see him riding the day like a horse until the trail of day leads him right into night. You suddenly find the peace of a horseback rider and the gift of discovery when quiet moments are honored.

Writing Time

What you are looking for: A poem that gives the reader a word picture of an ordinary moment or of a thought common to everyone.

To warm up before writing

1. Depending on the poem you choose, have students brainstorm topics to use: a common thought pictured, an ordinary moment, an object. It all depends on your choice of model.
2. Pick one example to practice with.
3. Help students decide what mood they want to paint.
4. Next, have them create some word pictures to show their example of an ordinary moment and its mood.
5. See if they can come up with a metaphor for the last line or even sooner if they desire. The last line needs to be strong and leave the reader with a new idea.

Assignment

1. Based on an idea from the model poem, choose what to write about.
2. Choose something you know about so that you can use details.
3. How can you make the reader see and feel the topic of your poem?
4. Create word pictures.
5. Make sure to use metaphors and similes.
6. Think about line length—should lines be short or long?

My Poem Based on "A Happy Birthday" by Ted Kooser

At the Coast

There is a moment when time hangs
caught between day and night
when you see the deer eating
but always alert, watchful, anticipating.

There is a moment when time hangs
and your vision pierces normal ways of seeing
like a telescope with a lens as big as the horizon
and your ears expand to take in a new universe of sound.

There is a moment when time hangs
caught on the antlers of a young buck
and you hear the wind swirling around you.
It fills you with bird wing sound,

the whispering of the leaves,
the spaces between them
and the secrets of root and earth.

Janice DeRuiter

Chapter Twelve
Using Silence to Enhance Observation

Oregon

❦

This lesson uses silence as a tool. By willing ourselves into silence, all our senses are freed. Inside the quiet, we hear and see from a new perspective. Like the students in Helen's classes, physical stillness adds to the ability to perceive in a new way. Line breaks, the poetic tool for this lesson, seem simple. Yet it is often the hardest thing for students to get. Either they just don't do them or they place them in whatever spot they feel like at the moment. So the same poem can have several different versions of line breaks. I always discuss line breaks in either the first or second workshop.

After many years of teaching, I have found that the following system works the best. I found this idea for teaching line breaks in an article titled "Meditations on White Spaces."[6] Type the model poem twice in large print. In one copy, the line breaks are there; in the other copy, there are no line breaks, and the poem has justified margins.

Explaining the Tools of Line Breaks and Stanzas

Line breaks control the rhythm of a poem. Longer lines slow the reader down. Shorter lines speed up the poem. Line breaks also create the shape a poem has on a page. One of the best uses of line breaks is to create a surprise for what comes next—make the reader wait for a new and wonderful image.

Stanzas in poetry act something like a paragraph in prose. They present another dimension to the poem's shape on the page. Stanzas are used when a poem shifts to a new image or mood or when a poet presents a new thought within the poem.

Before presenting the model poem, show your students a long poem with line breaks and stanzas. Turn the poem on its side so that the straight side is on the bottom. Ask them what shapes they see in the jagged edges. They usually come up with great images, saying it looks like a city, a mountain, or grass. Then show them an enlarged, justified version. Again ask them what it looks like. Now you will get answers like a block, a building, a skyscraper, or a rectangle.

Lesson Preparation

1. Either have copies of the model poem for each student or have it written where each student can see it.
2. Type the model poem twice using a large font—once with line breaks and stanzas and once without line breaks and stanzas and with justified margins.

---

[6] Tina Cane, "Meditations on White Spaces," *Teachers and Writers*, May–June 2003.

Presenting the Model Poem

The model poem is "Air" by William Stanley Merwin. You can access it at www.poemhunter.com/poem/air.

This poem is unusual and must be read aloud at least twice to really get into both its meaning and rhythm. I have used it successfully in classrooms. Although the poem is unusual when I ask students to tell me what setting Merwin is showing, I have found that they can articulate the scene to me. I always take students through each image so that I know they are "getting" it. Make sure they can discover the mood of the poem. I would look for words like "mystery" and "wonder." Make sure they can find the more visual metaphors, including "overturned lute" and "bundles of roads." There are other metaphors that both picture and add meaning. Look for "the leaves sitting in judgment" and "tomorrow, the blind man." Why do the curtains seem to have eyes? The ending gives the reader a desire to look deeper and feel deeper when outside in nature.

The next poem is "A Blessing" by James Wright.

Like the poem above, "A Blessing" ends with wonder. This poem encourages silence because to experience this scene a person has to be calm and still. The detail is vivid. This poem does not contain as much metaphor/simile as the previous poem; however, the reader is invited into the scene and can picture it easily. Because the main mission of a poem is to paint a word picture, this poem is a success. Midway through the poem, a simile shows both feeling and image: "They bow shyly as wet swans." Anyone who has spent time observing horses immediately knows the movement these two are making. More sensory detail is contained in the next simile: "And the light breeze moves me to caress her long ear/That is delicate as the skin over a girl's wrist." The season is expressly stated by the metaphor "young tufts of spring" referring to the grass. Again, make sure your students can articulate both the images presented here and the mood. Again, wonder drives this poem forward. The last two lines express this mood in a clear and surprising word picture. Peace and happiness breathe out of the poem as well.

Writing Time

What you are looking for: Vivid details of one scene showing season, mood, weather, and emotions using several senses and line breaks and, if the student chooses, stanzas.

There are several ways to give students something visual to look at so that they can come up with interesting details.

1. Go outside to just observe; leave the pencils and paper in the classroom. Come back inside to have the students write from what they've observed.
2. Hand out pictures of nature or use pictures available in a textbook.
3. Writing from memory is chancy. Students may not have enough details.
4. If you choose, have meditative, soothing, evocative music ready to play during writing time.

I try to take my students outside, even if it's raining. There are usually eaves you can stand under and still be able to observe what is outside. I pick a place that has the most "nature" in it, even if it is only some dirt, crumbled rocks, and dusty plants or a fence crawling with ivy. When teaching in Nebraska one winter, I had the students look out a window at the snow and ice, and we remembered scenes around town that each child was familiar with to come up with more details. What you are encouraging is silence and stillness as students focus on simply observing nature, noticing small details that we usually miss. Even if you stay inside, encourage silence. About three years ago, one student was awed by a simple dandelion in the grass and by the worm he noticed sheltering underneath it. He marveled that he'd never paid any attention to this bright yellow flower before.

Assignment: This long version of the assignment will help you give hints to students who are stuck.
1. Whether writing from outside images or from pictures, ask students to create a word picture of their "place."
2. Think about sky, weather, birds, sounds—anything you see or hear. If you're writing about the outdoors, the reader doesn't need to know you're at school.
3. How can you show the mood of where you are? What details do you need to make your reader see, smell, and hear the place?
4. How can you show the season?
5. How can you show your reader how you feel about this place?
6. What new thing can you show the reader about the discoveries that can be made when observing nature quietly?
7. Make sure you use a lot of details.
8. When you're done, look at line breaks, and add a slash symbol (/) if you feel the line should be broken somewhere besides where you first did it. (The / lines do not appear in the final poem.)
9. Can you use stanzas to show a change of image or to shape the rhythm?

The short version for students: At the simplest level, students are describing what they see, hear, and feel. They use that input to create their word pictures.

1. Remember what you experienced outside or look for details in your picture that will help you describe the place so that your readers can see, smell, and hear it in their minds.
2. Show the mood of your place, the season, and how you feel about it.
3. Try to create a word picture in your last line that *shows* something you discovered about nature today.
4. When you're done, check your line breaks for surprise. See if you want to add stanzas. See number eight above.

My Poem Based on a Discovery Made while Observing Nature in Silence

The Deer

His presence contains silence.
A silence so vast that you
can hear the stars move.

The gaze from his eyes
is a spear that pins
you onto the floor of the earth.

The stars, their movement,
his eyes and their piercing
remind your body of the earth's

spin and you discover your
body is circling, yet rooted
into place. Imagine

you have become as a planet
endlessly orbiting
the sun of your new world.

Janice DeRuiter

Chapter Thirteen
Inner Journey: Images from the Unconscious Mind

Northern California

Now that students have been introduced to metaphors, similes, and poetry's basics, they are ready to travel into the world of the unconscious mind. Taking this journey in a classroom requires some trickery. This lesson pulls students well away from the world of expository writing. On an inner journey, poets must let go of control and just let their poems flow out. To encourage students to let go of control, I try to create a dream machine in the classroom. During writing time, I play music and turn out the lights. For this series of lessons, I've included two different model poems. One uses house imagery, and the other uses water.

Often I choose not to use a model poem. Instead, I read poetry with the appropriate images while the students write. I allow them to grab a single word from a line. When they have enough words, they start their poems. If you have enough poetry on hand, this is a good technique and very different from the usual lesson. Lately, I have been making my own videos with suitable images, music, and a narrator reading poetry.

Lesson Preparation
What you'll need:
1. Copies of the model poem or a selection of poems to read
2. Dreamy music to play in the background.

Explaining the Unconscious Mind
For the purposes of this lesson, I approach the unconscious mind with a rather simple explanation. Think of a person's brain as having two levels. The conscious mind can be considered the top, where logical thought is born. This is the part of the mind that knows 4 + 4 = 8 and the part that lets you write a report on marine mammals. If it were a house, it would be the part you live in. But the unconscious mind is like the basement or attic where you store all kinds of unrelated memories and associations. These memories pop up at unexpected times. The one common experience we all have that comes out of our unconscious is dreams. Psychologists often talk about the meanings of dreams. Some of the things we dream about are universal symbols. You find these symbols in every culture. A symbol is something that stands for or represents another thing. To help the students understand, ask them what a dove stands for. I've never had a class yet that didn't know the answer: peace.

The following model poems contain images from two symbols—water and houses. Because I use dreams in the explanation, I always have to caution students that they are *not* writing about dreams. They must not say, "I fell asleep." or "I woke up." What the students are doing is freeing themselves to explore inside their own minds and to dare to go below the surface into the unconscious. This is a risk, but it is the place most good poetry comes from.

Introducing the Use of Active Verbs in Poetry

Both of the model poems presented below use descriptive, active verbs. This is a good opportunity to encourage their use. I would simply point them out after the model poem is read. It would break up the flow of this particular lesson to go into any more detail.

Presenting the Model Poem—Water

Before reading the model poem, I point out that water is a universal symbol and often shows up in dreams. Ask students to tell you why water is important enough that every culture would use it as a symbol. Hopefully, they will come up with answers showing that we need water to live, that our bodies are mostly water, that our planet is mostly water, and that life comes from water. So water, in general, is a symbol for life.

Snake Rhythms

A soft wind circles through the canyon,
swirls its melody side to side.
Tired people sink gently into the sand
and learn the gift of
the rhythm of the wind
and the ceaseless river flow.

River moments small and unexpected
creep into people's eyes,
seek out their inner songs
releasing them into
the rhythm of the wind
and the ceaseless river flow.

The river's changing flow pulls through
and into time, past its remembering
into an ever-shifting home
of uncertain place but everlasting peace,
the place of the rhythm of the wind
and the ceaseless river flow.

Janice DeRuiter

This poem deals not with water in general but with the experience of being on and near a river. As I wrote this, I found myself wanting to repeat lines. When I got down the images I wanted, I read through the poem and saw that I was setting up a pattern and trying to capture the soothing rhythm of a flowing river. So I capitalized on that. Each stanza has six lines and ends with the same two lines. The images show what can be learned when you stop and listen to a river. Go through each stanza and ask the students what they see and how they think the people in the poem are feeling. In the first stanza, it is the music of the wind and how people respond to the soft sand that captured my attention. All the stanzas illustrate what a watcher, a poet, can learn from a river. In the second stanza, the people, now completely enmeshed in river life, start to remember feelings and emotions they had forgotten. The last stanza shows the timelessness of rivers and the desire I discover to carry the feelings of peace with me wherever I go. Notice the descriptive verbs: "circles," "swirls," "sink," "creep," "seek," "pulls." Ask students what these verbs make them visualize. For review of line breaks, ask students which ones work the best for surprise. End by asking them what they think the river is a symbol for here. Hopefully they will have picked up on the word "peace" and the lines showing how rivers never stop flowing. This can lead into brainstorming about different bodies of water and their uses as symbols in the next section.

Writing Time

What you are looking for: A descriptive poem using some form of naturally occurring water. By the choice of details, the poem will create a mood and show an emotion. These details will also make clear to the reader what the image of water symbolizes in the poem.

After students have their writing materials ready to go, have them brainstorm different types of water: lakes, rivers, ponds, oceans, rain, floods, streams, waterfalls, etc. To get them thinking about water as a symbol or water as showing a mood, ask them what emotion a waterfall, for example, could show. Students usually come up with answers like "excitement," "nervous," or "happy." How could they use a waterfall and one of these emotions to create a metaphor about a person? One student came up with this response: "I am as happy as a waterfall dancing off a cliff into the ocean." If you feel they need it, practice with one more type of water, then give the assignment.

Assignment

1. Turn off the critic in your head. Don't worry about making sense. Just let words, ideas, and images pop out.
2. If you let each line be a word picture, you will end up saying something meaningful. The details you choose will create a mood.
3. Try to think about using water as a metaphor for an emotion. If you don't want to write about yourself, you can speak in the voice of someone else or give an objective description.
4. If you finish in time, see if you can replace some of your verbs with descriptive verbs.

Presenting the Model Poem—House

Before reading the model poem, talk about a house as a symbol. Ask students what the word "house" makes them think of. Then talk about the different rooms in a house and the associations we have with them. To target this discussion, remind students to think about what people do in each room. Talk about what emotions or moods can be represented by the various rooms. Next discuss the parts of a building that go into being a house—walls, doors, windows, even stairs. Again, what do walls do? What do windows do? A bedroom might be associated with rest or isolation. There is no right or wrong symbol for any given thing.

Stripping the Walls

It seems to me that parts of lives lie
in strips on the carpeted floor.
Or did the plaid of the wallpaper
jump
off these, patterned
walls just to decorate the floor?

Who knows?
Do I care?
The painter says he can strip the walls of paper
and paint them again
in just one day.

Imagine undoing all this agony in a few
Work-filled hours.

But I wonder when once the paper rockets,
the moons, the cowboys and Indians
have joined the plaid
on the floor of this room,

when once that's done,
will all this thick, dense
air disperse so I can breathe freely again?

Will all his anger, deceit, and twisted thoughts
give up what they've left behind?
Will they stay with him
in the jail that holds him now?
Will the air be clear?
Will I leave this door open once more to the light?

Poor painter,
a second day joined the first but now?
The room is sun-filled yellow and oh joy,
I can breathe again.

The door is open to welcome
any person who wishes to come inside.

Janice DeRuiter

This poem surprised me. Poems never obey the poet. They develop a life of their own. I set out to write a poem based on the poem "House" by Maya Angelou. Next thing I knew, my pen was back at my previous house and writing about this very difficult room. Like all poems written about private and disturbing moments, I struggled to craft it in language that everyone could relate to that was suitable for all ages. I wanted to share, but not too much. The transformation of the room that happened by simply stripping and painting the walls was almost life changing. No longer did I close the door to this room so that I didn't have to look inside. Now its door was open, inviting people in. That fact ended up being the surprise for me at the end of the poem. This is what writing out of the unconscious should do. It should surprise the poet as well as the reader. It took two different versions before I was happy with the poem. The first one was more controlled, in tight, two-line stanzas. That was way too much control for a poem about an out-of-control room. In both versions, the language is not dependent on comparisons but on description. This is unusual for me. But this poem and this room seemed to demand it. This room represented a time for me that was stark and real, and I don't think I could find metaphors to contain all that for me, at least not when writing about this particular room. Frankly, writing this paragraph has brought forth thoughts I'd not articulated before. I have talked a lot about my thought process because we are here dwelling in the world of the unconscious mind. As you have your students review this poem, make certain they can see the room and can understand about all the layers of wallpaper being taken off the walls. In this version, I do not stress the ages of the people the different types of paper represent. However, the descriptions of the papers give hints. See if students can articulate the different ages represented here and the progression of age.

Writing Time

What you are looking for: Poems using any part of a house to show an emotion or feeling

Assignment

1. Turn off the critic in your head. Don't worry about making sense. Just let words, ideas, and images pop out.
2. If you let each line be a word picture, you will end up saying something meaningful. The details you choose will create a mood.
3. Try to think about using a house and any of its parts as a metaphor for an emotion.
4. If you don't want to write about yourself, you can speak in the voice of someone else or give an objective description. You could even speak in the voice of the house.
5. If you finish in time, see if you can replace some of your verbs with descriptive verbs.

Chapter Fourteen
For Native American Worldview

Yurok Ceremonial Site, California

❦

If we look at the worldview of the Native American, we find another lens through which we can perceive the world around us. Studying the natural world and the people around us from a Native American point of view not only gives us a new view of our world; it also provides the poet with another world of rich imagery.

Because they have lived in close contact with nature, Native Americans observe natural cycles, which shape their belief system. I find that in presenting these beliefs to students, it's best to focus on one or two ideas rather than a complete overview. After traveling through many different forms, this lesson has settled on the approach of having students write about themselves and their heritage using precepts gleaned from Native American thought. I focus on an idea common to a Native American worldview. Being closely connected to nature, they often observe the cyclical nature of the natural world. For them, the repetitive cycles of the natural world illustrate the interconnectedness of all things.

Lesson Preparation

1. Prepare the model poem. Decide on your model poem. You can use the one I discuss or there are other suggestions at the end of the chapter. Decide how you want to present it to your students.
2. If there is an Indian tribe closely associated with your area, you might want to add some of their unique beliefs to this lesson.

Explaining the Native American Cyclical View

Part of being a poet is the willingness to discover more about yourself using points of view from other cultures. This lesson lets you think about who you are and who you want to be using a Native American view of life. Because of their close harmony with nature, Native Americans believe that the world of nature is as important as the human world. They observe that everything in nature seems to travel in circles. What kind of shape do the moon and the sun trace as they travel through the sky? What shape are the full moon and the sun? Ask students to name the four seasons in order. Have them repeat the order. What do the seasons form? A circle because the cycle never ends but keeps repeating. Then ask for someone to name the four directions. After the students answer, write the four directions on the board as they would appear on a map. Then join them by curved lines so that the resulting shape is a circle.

Presenting the Model Poem

For this lesson, model poems can be found on the Internet at various sites that feature Native American poetry. One I recommend is: http://www.hanksville.org/storytellers/

The poem I will focus on can be found at http://www.hanksville.org/storytellers/niatum/poems/SunSpinsDown.html. The poem is titled "Sun Spins Down but the Blue Jay Flies." Mr. Niatum is from the Klallam tribe and was born in Seattle, Washington. The Klallam are also referred to as "the Jamestown Band," which is part of the larger group we know as the Coast7. The site for the poem gives more information on Mr. Niatum. Here is the link http://www.hanksville.org/storytellers/niatum/. Mr. Niatum also maintains the following web page. The link is http://members.authors-guild.net/dniatum/

For the purpose of this lesson, it is necessary to know that the Salish religion was both shamanistic and animistic. Shamans were the mediators between the natural world and the spirit world. Animism is the belief that natural phenomena possess spirits.

The Salish believe in guardian spirits, which are acquired by vision quests. Spirits live either in the land of the dead or in animate or inanimate objects. The guardian spirit dance is held in winter. It is interesting to note that the suggested model poem is set in winter. While I can't know this for certain without hearing it from the poet, it feels to me like his guiding spirit might be a mountain. The Pacific Northwest's primary landscape features are mountains. There are two mountain ranges there: the Coast Range and the Cascade Range. Near Seattle are Mt. Rainier, Mt. St. Helens, Glacier Peak, and Mt. Baker.

As you read through this poem with your students, help them to see that the poet references the cycle of seasons and also the cycles of moon and life. The latter is brought in by the reference to the poet's grandfather. Be aware also of the mystery the poem contains. It doesn't explain itself completely but relies rather on impressions the reader forms while reading and feeling its images and journeying with the poet as he travels through the seasons with the mountain as a teacher.

By the imagery used in the first stanza, the poet suggests that there is a feeling that leads to a guide showing the way to earth and also to the guardian. In the second stanza, the poet presents this guide as the mountain he calls "grandfather." The mountain is both animate and inanimate to the poet. The presence of this mountain has guided the poet's life. It is the looming immensity that covers his days.

By stanza 3, the poet is feeling calmed by the presence of the mountain. Winter is passing away and is heading toward the renewal of spring. As sky keeper completes the "winter phase," the poet feels that he will find what he is searching for and that it will speak to him in a calming voice. It is interesting to me that calmness is expressed as both the voice of snow and the voice of thunder. Thunder isn't usually depicted as a calm presence. Both of these things would be part of life experienced in the presence of a mountain. Here we find a total acceptance of nature as it is and a willingness to listen to the lessons nature can show.

Writing Time

What you are looking for: A poem that shows what the poet considers to be his or her guide in life. The poem should show something of what the poet is hoping to find by following the guide. This guide also should be able to show something about the poet as a person. The guide chosen should be something in nature or even someone very important to the poet. The poem should not explain but *show* what is important to the poet so that the reader has to discover what is behind the imagery.

Assignment

Basic task: Show what you can learn from nature by allowing yourself to be taught by a natural guide. This guide can be an animal or a feature of the landscape like a mountain or tree.

1. Before starting to write, brainstorm on some part of the natural world that is important to you.
2. What do you think you learn from or could learn from this guide if you listened carefully? Show this; don't simply tell your reader.
3. As you write, try to have each line contain a word picture.
4. Go get details, bring in seasons and the cycles of moon and sun. You could even use the circle formed by the four directions.
5. To get yourself started, feel free to use the single line followed by stanzas that Mr. Niatum uses. Find a phrase for yourself like the poem's first line and let it stand alone to start the first image.

Suggestion for another model poem:

John E. Smelcer, ed., *Durable Breath: Contemporary Native American Poetry* (Anchorage, Alaska: Salmon Run Press, 1994).

This anthology has many fine poems in it. I especially recommend "An Indian Walks in Me" by Marilou Awiaka, Cherokee, and "Pull" by Duane BigEagle, Osage.

My Poem Based on Duane Niatum's "Sun Spins Down but the Blue Jay Flies"

Of Trees, Leaves, and Eyes at Sunset
I wish for you

a moment out of time
a drawing in of rock and leaf
of intersection with a tree

a gift like this of finding
a green world that speaks
only to you

and tells you truths
you never knew you needed.

In my moment I found
madrone and its worlds

of leaves with eyes of gold
that spoke silent secrets at sunset
about a wisdom that keeps me

knowing that I am but a part
of all these many worlds

the universes of grass,
the planets of bird songs,
and this dwelling place on a rock

where my willing silence

leaves me open to hear the hum
of the setting sun

leaves me open to feel the comfort
in the circle of hill, rock, tree, flower, and grass

leaves me peaceful as twilight becomes night
and the circle of days bids me come again

to find a tree and bind myself again
in a company that is always there waiting.

Janice DeRuiter

Chapter Fifteen
For Collaborative Writing:
Renga/Rengay

Peach Blossom, Northern California

As the mind of a poet expands outward, it not only dwells on other people, but it strives to understand other cultures as well. As a counterweight to the American tendency to approach life from an individualistic point of view, I have introduced students to two cooperative forms of Japanese poetry called Renga and Rengay. We discussed Renga in Chapter Five. But what is a Rengay? To understand Rengay, you will have to cope with a very abbreviated and simplified history of Japanese linked verse. If you find yourself wanting to know more, several books are listed in the bibliography that go into this subject in much more detail.

Renga

To give themselves a form of poetry that was more spontaneous, the Japanese created linked verses. These verses were related to each other by common elements, and each verse was created by a group of poets taking turns. The form is called Renga. Renga is more a game than a poetic form. Rengas were created at a Renga party. They used detailed observation of natural objects. There would be a starting verse called "Hokku." Then each guest would write a three-line stanza. Sometimes as many as one thousand stanzas were written. As mentioned in Chapter Five, Bashō, a great Japanese poet who lived from1644 to 1694, preferred thirty-six stanzas. A Renga is image-filled. The reader must have something to look at, taste, smell, and touch. A Renga has the characteristics of spontaneity, improvisation, and fun. The stanzas are linked by writing an image suggested by the previous stanza. This image can be a parallel or similar image, a contrasting image, a shift in focus, or a link with words from a previous stanza. It can repeat sounds, repeat a word, play off a word in the previous stanza, or use an association with a previous word. It also can have a contrasting mood. The Renga should not use emotion words. An emotion or mood can be shown by the word pictures chosen. And there are still more rules. The starting verse should have season and place. Stanzas alternate between three and two lines usually: short–long–short, followed by long–long.

As Renga progressed, the starting verses, Hokku, that were not used began to be collected on their own. The leftover Hokku became Haiku. Haiku poems have three lines using an object, a season, and a place, in any order. The third line should present a new insight.

Rengay

As Renga continued to be practiced, there were many variations on the form. I will not go into all of them here. Leap forward now to the year 1992. An American, Garry Gay, created a form called "Rengay." This form was kept relatively simple so that poets could create a linked verse while doing another activity like taking a walk. A Rengay has a theme, and its links are provided by the theme or by the images used. A Rengay depends on a moment in time that the two or three poets have in common. Each stanza of a Rengay should be able to stand on its own. Here are the rules:

1. Six stanzas are written by two or three poets.
2. The poem has to capture a single experience common to each of the writers so that it has one theme or topic. It does not tell a story but captures a moment in word pictures.
3. Like a Renga, it contains no emotion or opinion words.
4. It should be set in the season during which the experience happens.
5. There are six stanzas, formed as follows:
   Stanza 1: Three lines of short–long–short
   Stanza 2: Two Lines of long–long
   Stanzas 3 and 4: Three lines of short–long–short
   Stanza 5: Two lines of Long–long
   Stanza 6: Three lines of short–long–short
   The "formula" looks like this: 1-3, 2-2, 3-3, 4-3, 5-2, 6-3.
6. The links between verses cannot be repeated words. The reader should have to think to discover the links. That's part of the fun.
7. The links can be repeated sounds, or one poet can refer to what someone else has written but must present it in a different way because Rengays are about a common experience that links the verses together as well.

After I discovered the Rengay, I no longer presented the Renga. In my opinion, the Rengay provides a form that is more accessible for students, so that will be the focus here. In researching Rengay, I have discovered that there are as many different sets of "rules" as there are authors. What remains the same is the number of stanzas, the unifying theme, and the requirement that two to three poets contribute stanzas. Technically, the number of stanza lines changes depending on whether there are two or three poets. For classroom use, it's easier to settle on one variation with the understanding that if the Rengay is written with fewer stanzas or more or the wrong number of lines, it is not a problem because the form is so fluid.

Lesson Preparation

1. Decide how to present the model poem. You could just read it.
2. Decide how you will divide up the group. Because numbers are rarely equal, you will probably have some groups of two and some of three. I have become very undemocratic when dividing students into groups for writing. When students complain that they can't work with the assigned partner, I go into a short speech about cooperative writing. One important part of the lesson is to learn to work with people.

Presenting Rengay

Much of this is a repeat from the Introduction but in an abbreviated form for students.

To give themselves a freer use of poetry, to be spontaneous and improvise, Japanese created linked verses. These verses were related to each other by common elements. A different poet created each verse. The form is called Renga. Bashō (1644–1694) preferred a Renga of thirty-six stanzas rather than one thousand. The rules for linking the verses were quite strict. We won't go through all the variations that followed. The value of this form of poetry is that it requires several poets to cooperate. Because, as Americans, we tend to do things as individuals, this is a new way of writing for us.

Leap forward to the year 1992 here in the United States. An American, Garry Gay, created a form of linked verse called "Rengay." A Rengay is written by two or three poets using a common experience for the unifying theme. The common experience should capture a single moment. A Rengay has six stanzas that follow this pattern: 1-3, 2-2, 3-3, 4-3, 5-2, 6-3. I do not insist that each stanza be able to stand on its own. But as you will see in the model poem, when this happens, it makes the resulting poem even more amazing.

Presenting the Model Poem

Finding the Model Poem

http://haikuworkshop.pbwiki.com/RengayThroughTheSeasons

Go to the above website. There you will find a chart with Rengays listed by date first, collaborators (if any,) season, and title. I recommend the following three: September 2–8, 2007, "Popsicle Stick"; December 30, 2007–January 5, 2008, "Below a Drift"; and August 10–16, 2008, "A Rosy Shade."

Choose your favorite and present it to the class. The writers have made these easy to present. After each title, there is a link to notes that tell you exactly what the links between stanzas are.

Writing Time

What you are looking for: Each Rengay should follow a common theme showing a place or describing a common experience. Each student should have participated in writing the Rengay. The Rengays should not tell about going somewhere, for instance, but should show the place. Be aware that there can be a very successful Rengay that does not follow the rules about number of lines and stanzas.

Before you write: Divide the students into groups. Make sure they put *all* of their names on the paper. It helps, too, if you know who wrote each stanza.

Assignment

1. Decide on an experience to write about. It must be something everyone in the group has done and/or a place everyone has seen.
2. When you write, all writers must cooperate and do their best to follow the form.
3. Remember: You are showing one moment in time with description *only*, no emotion or opinion words, and you are *not* telling a story.
4. Decide who will write the first stanza. Then proceed clockwise.
5. Formula for Rengay:
   Stanza 1 = 3 lines
   Stanza 2 = 2 lines
   Stanza 3 = 3 lines
   Stanza 4 = 3 lines
   Stanza 5 = 2 lines
   Stanza 6 = 3 lines
6. Remember: Links between stanzas cannot be repeated words.
7. The season and its images can help you think of links.
8. A stanza can link to one several stanzas above it.
9. When you are done, go back over your Rengay to make sure the number of lines in each stanza is correct and that you have six stanzas.

Links to poems and explanations:
http://haikuworkshop.pbwiki.com/RengayThroughTheSeasons

Explanations of Rengay on the web:
This link is from Garry Gay, who created the Rengay form:
www.brooksbookshaiku.com/ggayweb/rengay.html

This link goes into a detailed explanation of Rengay and has links to other sites:
www.baymoon.com/~ariadne/form/rengay.htm

Chapter Sixteen
Writing to Understand: Empathy and Voice

Sorrento, Italy

Poets observe more than just what is visible in the world around them. Having the mind of a poet means developing the ability to understand what goes on inside of people. It means imagining their lives and taking the time to notice all of the small details that make them individuals. In a classroom setting, I've been able to have students grasp this essential idea by studying photos and art of people as they appear in real life.

For this lesson, I use a collection of magazine and newspaper photographs and art postcards showing people's faces. Whenever I receive a magazine or a newspaper, I keep in mind the need for photographs to jump-start students. Museums are a great source for art postcards that can be purchased in booklets. The Internet is a vast resource and has the added advantage of being free. In Google™, for example, type in "images + person" or "images + faces/people." Typing in "art + faces" pulls up some unique results.

Encouraging Empathy Using Photographs: Lesson Preparation
1. Decide how you will present the model.
2. Gather photographs showing people's faces. Newspapers and magazines are excellent sources, as is the Internet.

Explaining the Use of Empathy and Voice in Poetry
Empathy means the ability to put yourself in another's place and to try to understand their feelings and their life. You are writing to find the good in the person and to understand and value their life. When you put yourself in another's place, you are often surprised by your own ideas. For me, writing to understand others is one of the paramount tasks of a poet. As you observe and write, you come to a new perception about the person and often about people in general. Writing out of empathy increases your observation skills and your ability to make unusual connections. There are several ways to write a poem about another. This introduces the subject of the "voice" of the poem. You can write as the objective observer looking at this person with no mention of "I" or "you." The model poem presents this voice. This is a good way to preserve your impressions of a person. It is more in-depth than a mere photo. Or you can write using another's voice. You can actually become the person in the picture. Writing as someone other than yourself is often very freeing because it lets you leave self behind. Or you can write as the observer using the first person.

Presenting the Model Poem

For this lesson, I am using a poem I wrote myself because I know the thought process behind the poem. When we were in Greece several years ago, I became aware of all the widows from World War II still wearing black for their dead husbands and sons. At their advanced age, their faces had become maps. Fellow tourists seemed to have no problem violating their privacy and taking pictures. I simply couldn't do that. As I strolled on the concrete wharf of the island of Aegina, I became aware of this wonderful woman sitting in front of her house. I observed her as carefully and as discretely as possible, then rushed back to our boat to capture her in my journal. The following poem is the result. As you go through this poem, use it to review the poetic tools you have covered so far.

Sculpture

An immobile woman sits framed
by an open door. Black dress
stark against the white house
with its vivid blue shutters. Her eyes
lock onto the sea. Years
have pulled on her face
until her cheekbones are mountains
and sunken cheeks, valleys. Dark eyes
peer out from caves
in the cliff of her face.

To be Greek is to endure
here until your face becomes
an island. As the summer's heat
dries all your days, you watch
ancient temples crumble
listen to gods' voices lament
in falling fluted marble.

Janice DeRuiter[7]

Notice that my poem starts out with very concrete details as I try to paint with words the lady and her surroundings. How does the first line break work for surprise? What does the verb "lock" imply? I use several metaphors in a row to describe her face. Ask students what they picture from these images. Why do I say her eyes "peer out from caves?" See if

---

[7] Janice DeRuiter, "Sculpture," *New Works Review* 5, no. 4.

students can visualize how her face's bone structure has become more prominent as the harsh Greek sun ages her. Ask for student opinions about the mood of this woman. How do they think she's feeling as she sits there? Have students find the descriptive verbs in the first stanza.

See if students understand why I put the stanza break where I did. I use the second stanza to take the poem beyond this woman to what it means to be Greek. Ask them to find the metaphors in this stanza as well. Make sure they understand that the Greek landscape is dotted with ancient ruins made of marble. For more review, see if they can find all the alliteration and assonance. (Remind students if necessary that alliteration is repetition of beginning sounds and assonance is the repetition of interior sounds.) I use assonance frequently in this poem, not just with vowels but with consonants. The long vowels and consonants lengthen the sound of the lines. Point out that all my images come from the Greek landscape. I wrote this poem strictly for my own enjoyment. But it has been presented several times in public settings. Listeners who have lived in Greece tell me that I did capture what it means to be an elderly woman in Greece. If I did, that is the result of writing to understand. The poem surprised me when it came to the point that said "finished."

Before students begin to write, use a picture of a person to practice on. Walk it around the room and ask students for images to describe the person. A black and white picture of Albert Einstein standing outside looking up at something is one of my favorites to use. I never tell students who is in the picture. Most years, I get lucky, and someone will describe him as looking up at the sky wondering what is there. Some years a whole class will get stuck on commenting about how fat he is. That kind of comment does give me an excellent opportunity to point out the need to be positive when describing a person.

Writing Time

What you are looking for: The poem produced for this lesson should describe a person and the surrounding scene from an empathetic point of view. The poems should use metaphor and simile. By describing a person with sensitive detail, the poet should show something about the person's feelings and life.

Assignment

1. Imagine being face to face with the person in your picture. What can you discover from studying his or her face? Be positive.
2. Try to imagine the person's mood.
3. Describe the person using detail.
4. Show the setting.

5. Is there anything in the setting that adds to your information about this individual?
6. What is the most unusual thing about the person in your picture? How can you show that using comparisons?
7. What images do you think of to describe the person?

Think about what this face has to teach you about the person's life.

Here are some suggestions of poems from the Internet about people and observation:

"People" by Jean Toomer
http://famouspoetsandpoems.com/poets/jean_toomer/poems/17905.html

"A Blind Woman" by Ted Kooser
http://www.poetryfoundation.org/archive/poem.html?id=171356

"Old Folks Laugh" by Maya Angelou
http://oldpoetry.com/opoem/94131-Dr--Maya-Angelou-Old-Folks-Laugh

Chapter Seventeen
Self in Context: Poetry of Place

Sonoma Coast, California

🌿

The mind of a poet develops in and is influenced by the place called home. This home may be a landscape from childhood or the place where the poet was happiest. And, yes, it can be the current home, the streets or land traveled every day. The reader can discern the effects on a poet's imagery of the world around him or her. Some writers are so identified with the landscape of their poetry that it is difficult to think of them separately. Think of Robert Frost and his New England farm or of John Steinbeck and the region of California's Monterey Bay. Pablo Neruda's poetic images are grounded in the rocky, coastal landscape of Chile. A lesson based on a place the writer knows well carries with it special challenges. Because the place is well known, a poet often assumes his or her readers know more than they do. So the challenge is to write in vivid detail so the reader is with the poet inside this place. In focusing on a place, a poet has to be able to convey what makes this particular place worthy of a poem. Readers need that moment of wishing they could visit this "home" the poet speaks of with such clarity and longing. When the poet is crafting images, the reader must realize constantly that the images convey visual imagery as well as the mood or feel of the place.

Lesson Preparation

1. The model poem I discuss here is "The Changing Light" by Lawrence Ferlinghetti. You can find it at www.poets.org; type in the title and poet's name. Make sure students can see the poem because the shape on the page is part of the poem's appeal.
2. Be ready to review all of poetic tools covered in this series of lessons. Go through the model poem and find the metaphors, similes, sound similarities, and descriptive verbs for yourself.

Explaining the Use of Place as Poetic Image

Showing the mood of a place is a difficult task, especially for student poets. For this reason, I put this lesson near the end of a poetry workshop. When introducing this lesson, your basic responsibility is to have your students understand the importance of showing either where they live or another favorite place in a new way, with an artist's eyes. Remind them that all writers invariably give readers clues about the place where the poet lives by the images they choose. Explain the importance of understanding ourselves within the context of where we live. This lesson and model help emphasize how the shape of a poem on the page adds to the reader's perception of the mood of the poem. The shape also helps the reader understand the poet's approach in framing the images of this particular poem.

Presenting the Model Poem

When reviewing "The Changing Light" by Lawrence Ferlinghetti, begin by asking students how the shape of the poem adds to the meaning. Help them notice that the lines drift across the page like the city drifts "anchorless upon the ocean." If the poem were in formal four-line stanzas with an alternating rhyme scheme, how would the reader perceive the poem? Would the images of the city drifting seem as visual to the reader? The lack of punctuation contributes to the sense of "drifting." The lines contain no finality, only the stopping of the visual impact on the page as a break leads you to another line and another image. Notice how the poet creates his own "form" by using the same format for each stanza: first line capitalized and set at the left margin, and the other lines coming in with different insets. What image does Ferlinghetti use to unify the poem? Of course, Ferlinghetti sets the reader up to track the differences in light by the title. If your students are not familiar with San Francisco, you might show them how it perches on the edge of the ocean so that it has the appearance of an island, especially when driving across one of the bridges that link it to the communities across the bay. Ferlinghetti contrasts the light of San Francisco to other places the reader may have been or at least seen pictures of. He uses the changing times of day to further color his painting of the different lights seen in San Francisco. The word "halcyon," meaning untroubled, peaceful, and quiet, adds to the reader's impression of the city. He uses the word "veil" to refer to evening light and then follows that with a line describing the night fog as "scrim," which is tightly woven cotton. The scrim of night fog creates another "veil" that covers the city. Four lines after the poet uses the word "veil," he uses the word "vale." This vale, a valley of light, holds the city as it "drifts/anchorless upon the ocean." With his ending image, what is the poet comparing the city to? Imagine a ship of buildings floating in the fading light of evening.

Now that your students have seen the model poem, have them brainstorm on the moods a place can show. Ask them to picture a place *outside* that they know very well. Discourage the use of backyards, athletic fields, or school grounds. We are using the whole of a place where they live. For example, I grew up in a southern California desert canyon. Even now, when I climb and cling to rocks, I feel a sense of home. Any canyon tends to pull me in and invite me to stay. If you are able, share your "home" geography and its effect on you. Draw your students out so that they understand the effect of weather, time of day, buildings, landscape, vegetation, city elements, and even the people on the mood of a place. Refer back to the model poem so they notice the details used there and how the author added mood to the poem.

Help students see that all of the poetic techniques they have learned so far will help them craft their poetic picture of a place. A lengthy discussion isn't required. Students should have a clear grasp by now of the basic elements of poetry. Just be sure they remember details, word pictures, metaphor, and simile. Remind them, too, of the value of free association, descriptive verbs, and sound similarities in shaping mood. Ferlinghetti uses most of these techniques in his poem. This review should take up only a few minutes of your time and can be done as you read the model poem. The main task for this lesson is, of course, writing a poem.

Writing Time

What you are looking for: A poem that, through its use of description, imagery, and shape, paints the look and feel of a particular place important to the poet. The poem should have a visual impact on the reader as the student uses line breaks and placement on the page to add to the mood.

Assignment
1. Decide what place you'll describe using images, not facts.
2. Think about what makes this place different from another.
3. What is the landscape like? What characteristics make it unusual? What is important to you? Show this in word pictures.
4. Your first couple of lines should tell or show the reader where you are.
5. Choose details carefully, using only the most vivid ones. Remember, you can add to details by picturing the place at different times of day and in different types of weather.
6. Let the shape of the poem reflect the feel of the place.
7. Focus on descriptive verbs and find comparisons to evoke your sense of place.
8. End with a strong image to pull your poem together.

My Poem Based on the Canyon of My Childhood

The Canyon Still Sounding
mica flecked in warm quartz
cool granite stream
showers of shale spires falling
chips of running fools
gold safe in caves
nobody can see
the small round ball child
a brave cowboy
curled protecting her hoard
inside this world
where everything is
streams river falls spring
willow lace and cactus pinchushion
lizard snake horses

on the rim
the barn hides kittens in the straw
they watch the saddle
on the sawhorse buck the rider off
the sawhorse snorts
when I fall
the bridles clink in laughter

when the hay comes in
I ride it to the loft
sleep on a fresh bale
the wind sounds off the granite
rustles willow leaves and oak
remember remember

Janice DeRuiter[8]

[8] Janice DeRuiter, "The Canyon Still Sounding," *Listen to Me* (New York: The Geryon Press Limited, 1991), 81.

Chapter Eighteen
Risk and the Imagination

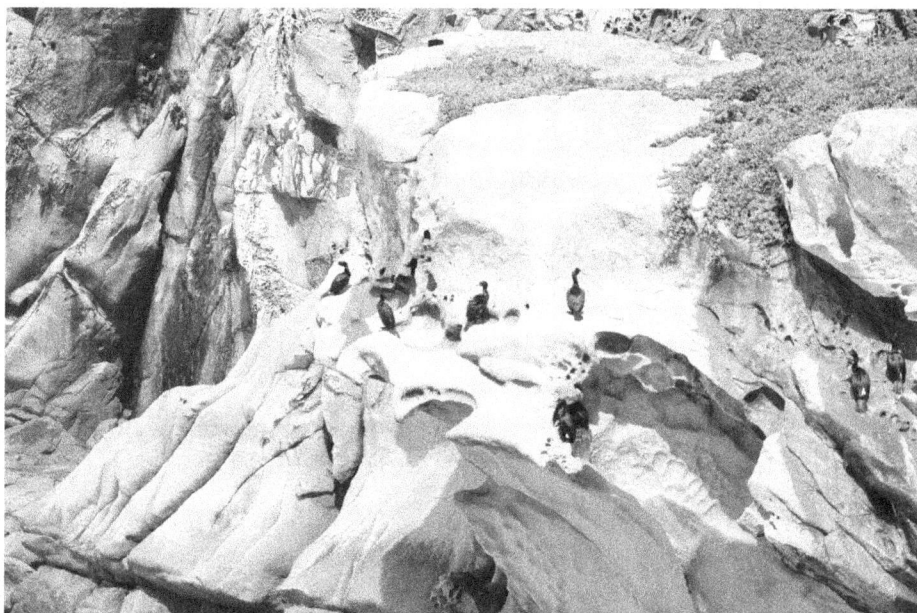

Sonoma Coast, California

For this lesson, I use the poetry of Wallace Stevens. I will present a few details about him in the section for students. Stevens's poetry focuses on surprising imagery and subjects. For me, he is the perfect poet to help students look at images in a whole new way. His poetry encourages the reader to leave behind any norms of thought. Stevens illustrates how paying attention to the smallest details about a thing can change a poet's perspective. The style of the model poem, "Thirteen Ways of Looking at a Blackbird," works well with a lesson that follows fairly closely on the heels of Renga or Rengay. This poem also provides a fresh look at the use of stanzas to show a new image or idea.

Lesson Preparation

1. Access the model poem, "Thirteen Ways of Looking at a Blackbird" by Wallace Stevens at www.poets.org by typing in the author's name and poem's name.
2. Decide how to present the model poem.
3. Collect pictures of animals in a natural setting with only one animal in each picture.
4. Before writing time, practice extending the image by adding adjectives, details of the setting, and active verbs. Encourage the use of free association

Explaining Risk and the Imagination

Poets and their poetry use creativity, the imagination, to look at the ordinary in a new way. They open their minds to surprising images. These images can scare you because you sense that you've never thought this way before. As you allow these ideas to surface, your poetry shifts into a different place, and you create comparisons that are fresh and unusual.

One of the ways to encourage the arrival of these new images is to pay attention to the smallest detail of your subject. This close attention to detail is one of the main tasks of the poet.

The American poet Wallace Stevens used this attention to detail in his poetry. His poetry shows how focusing your mental attention on each individual part of your subject leads to unusual writing and a shift in how you look at each thing. Stevens shows that there are no set rules about who is and who can be a poet. Wallace Stevens was a lawyer who worked in the insurance industry. Stevens composed poems as he walked to and from the office in his town of Hartford, Connecticut. This is not the usual life we imagine for a poet.

As we read his poem, "Thirteen Ways of Looking at a Blackbird," you can easily see his relationship to the style we used when we wrote Rengays. The stanzas of this poem use techniques similar to Haiku. The changes in imagery between the stanzas give you an excellent example of how stanzas help a poem show its shifts in word pictures.

Presenting the Model Poem

Before reading the model poem with the students, ask them to pay close attention to what Stevens is doing in this poem at the simplest level. As they read, ask them to picture each image in the poem so they can describe it in their own words.

This poem is just plain fun. It takes the image of a blackbird and plays with it until the blackbird expands in your mind into something huge and magnificent. Have students go through the poem stanza by stanza. Help them with some of the words that may puzzle them. Remind them that they are to look for what Stevens did in this poem at the simplest level. Ask them what they visualize for each verse. Help them find the similes and metaphors. As you read through the poem together, look for other poetic tools. You'll find assonance and alliteration, as well as active verbs and detailed description. Think of questions to ask that will help your students picture these unusual images. I like to draw out the reasoning behind the image of three blackbirds equaling three minds for the tree. If there are three blackbirds each has a mind so Wallace can have a tree with three minds. Notice the false logic of stanza 4. Stanza 5 sets up a list of things the poet likes. At the end of the list, you get the silence that follows when the blackbird finishes whistling. Regarding stanza 6, ask them what they think barbaric glass looks like. See if someone realizes the hint of fear presented here by the shadow of the blackbird pacing to and fro. I like the fun in stanza 7 of making the blackbirds seem more worthy of attention than golden birds. Stanza 8 shows clearly how important blackbirds are for the poet inside this poem. For stanza 9, have the students imagine they are flying and that on the ground below them, circles are marked out. As they fly, they cross the outlines of the circles. Stanzas 10 and 11 present scenarios that are not possible, but the reader can still picture them. Stanza 11 sets up a feeling of fear again using the image of blackbirds. Stanza 12 sets up false logic like stanza 4 does. The poem ends as it began, with an unusual image for the reader to puzzle over and enjoy. Stanza 13 is perhaps the most grounded in reality. Kindly, Stevens lets his readers rest at the end of this poem in a place they can clearly imagine. Make sure your students see how disconnected each stanza is from the one that precedes it. The only connection among them all is the image of blackbirds. The content varies wildly from stanza to stanza.

Ask students if they understand everything they read. See how they feel about so many impossible things being presented as fact.

By now, students should grasp that Stevens uses a new way of looking in each stanza of this poem. He forces his reader to confront a changed perception of blackbirds in every image he presents. Never again will a blackbird be simply a glossy black bird. It will be something fearful, elaborate, and mysterious all at the same time.

If you feel your students are ready, ask them to pay attention to the changes in voice scattered throughout the poem. Some are written in the first person, with the poet speaking in his own voice. Other stanzas are written in the third person, with the poet speaking as an objective observer.

Writing Time

What you are looking for: Students should write a poem about only one animal or event. They should provide the reader with details so that the scene or animal can be visualized. In their poem, they should try to get beyond the surface and show the reader the feeling that the subject of the poem evokes in the poet. They should use stanzas and come up with new ways of looking at their chosen subject.

Before starting to write: To give students something visible to look out, try to give each student a picture of an animal in nature. Go over the assignment. Perhaps have them repeat it back to you in their own words to make sure they understand what they're doing.

Assignment

1. At the simplest level, write a poem in which you show an animal or event in several different ways.
2. In each stanza, use a new idea, a shift in description, and/or a change in voice.
3. Free yourself to ask questions that have no real answers.
4. Look for what strikes you as strange or unusual.
5. Make the reader look at the ordinary in a new way, with new eyes.
6. Suggestions: You can show your subject at different times of day, in relation to unusual things. You can use it to show emotions. If you use an animal, put your animal in different places and situations. Use free association. Surprise yourself. Be free.

My Poem Based on "Thirteen Ways of Looking at a Blackbird"

Ten Ways of Looking While Walking

I

hot western summer
green reeds mark
the absent stream
they learn to meander like water

II

heat sends dogs and me out early
we meet new people
enjoy arching willow and cattails tracing a stream
all still in the hot air

III

hot western summer
ducks glide in,
rest on shrinking pond
water plants flourish
in warm shallow water

IV

by the pond
a dead tree
yet alive
a great egret
bright in the bare interwoven branches

V

egret stands a sharp white
against the emerald green rice field
when the great bird rises on the hot dense air
it stops time

VI

a half moon faces east
looks forward to sunrise
as sun sets it etches
the dry hills with golden light

VII

cold air slams
into summer
grey sky dulls golden grass
cold lets old energized dog forge onto the sidewalk
with small fast legs

VIII

walking nearly night
moon slivered in a western sky
warmth floats on the skin
autumn's announced arrival
drowned out by summer

IX

frost defines the morning
afternoon the sun changes that definition
sun slants across the hills
makes them golden, warm

X

dog walk
forthright bright after rain
the sky and air
shout autumn
morning joy
breathing we walked
into a mind and heart of silence

Janice DeRuiter

Index

www.ingramcontent.com/pod-product-compliance
Lightning Source LLC
Chambersburg PA
CBHW061738020426
42331CB00006B/1284